Beyond
Individualism

<u>**Other Quest books by Dane Rudhyar**</u>

Occult Preparations for a New Age
Culture, Crisis, and Creativity

Cover art by

Jane A. Evans

Beyond Individualism

The Psychology of Transformation

Dane Rudhyar

*This publication made possible with
the assistance of the Kern Foundation*

The Theosophical Publishing House
Wheaton, Ill. U.S.A.
Madras, India/London, England

Library of Congress Cataloging in Publication Data
Rudhyar, Dane, 1895-
Beyond individualism.
(A Quest book)
Includes index.
1. Spiritual life. 2. Self-realization.
3. Theosophy. I. Title.
BL624.R79   128   78-64906
ISBN 0-8356-0518-3

To John White
In Appreciation and Friendship

CONTENTS

FOREWORD

Rudhyar and I have become friends by a series of concentric events. He lived next door one summer. We met at conferences. We had friends in common who founded a bookstore based on his ideas. My wife painted a cover for one of his novels. We had dinner a few times. The usual seemingly random way that people meet in this world.

His books I approached very slowly. I had no special attraction or knowledge of astrology, so I was not drawn to the books he's written in that area. I'm not a musician so I hadn't realized that he was a composer as well as a writer about music. Philosophy had been effectively reduced to tedium by my professors in that subject so I shied away from those books of his as well.

The novel my wife worked on I read on a cross-country flight. It was apparently a science-fiction story (*Return from No Return*) but there was something added, like a counter-melody or a subtle harmonic. At one point in the book I found my eyes filling with tears. What do you do on a 747 when you are reading and crying to yourself? You feel embarrassed, surprised; you crouch down low in your seat and hope no one will ask to help you or comfort you.

What had moved me? Rudhyar had touched on a theme that was so universal and so personal that for an instant I was awakened from my narrow point of view and saw the larger framework in which I (and you) are embedded. It was a shock, not a re-cognition, but a re-collection, of being brought together again, of realigning my personal position with the larger flow of events and energy in which my life moves.

Return from No Return did this in a gentle, lulling way. It is clearly fiction; it's about some other people in some other frame of reference, much of it on other worlds. It sings along with all the music and good cheer that is allowed to science-fiction, or philosophy-fiction writers. There is no direct warning—"THIS BOOK MAY BE DANGEROUS TO YOUR COMPLACENCY" written on the outside spine, nothing to alert my normal academic and rational defensiveness.

Realizing that I'd been tricked into a moment of wakefulness, I thought again about Rudhyar's books and what he is doing.

It now looks to me as if he has been engaged in the usually unpopular task of awakening people to their own place in the scheme of things. What looks like a wide range of interests and a wide span of publications has truly been a wide range of gift-wrappings of the same message.

He told me once that the nice part of writing astrological columns about the birthdates and charts of famous persons is that you could discuss anything you felt was important about the person as long as you rooted your remarks within the frame of the chart. He could ask his readers to reflect on whatever was important for him and still fulfill their needs to see it as "mere" astrology if they wished. So when Rudhyar gave me the first part of this book to read I was partly warned, partly wary of this man and his ideas.

This book is not gift-wrapped, there is no disguise, no cheerful fictional narrative, no astrological conundrums, no musical interludes. It is the facts of the case explicitly delineated and forcefully presented.

The only device that Rudhyar has used is to call it a psychology. I am a psychologist. Correction—my degree is in psychology and I have read and written most extensively within those borders. I think "psychologically", I suggest that others can benefit from psychology and so forth. I thought, in looking at this title, that Rudhyar has turned his attention to my discipline, my bite of the original apple. It would be easy and relaxing for me to involve myself in his reflections on my turf.

Damn! Tricked again. I think I'm writing this to forewarn you that he has done it once more.

This book is not a book which will come to rest within psychology. It is a book which *redefines* psychology, stretches it far beyond its narrow, conventional, academic and complacent limits. It is about understanding humanity and its relation to the earth.

Let me give you a feeling of what that is about. There is a film "Powers of Ten"—which gives its viewers a sense of context, a sense of realistic proportion about their place in the universe. A sequence shows a person; then you rise above the person and see an area ten times larger than the person, say a section of beach with other people; then you go up again to another ten-fold expansion. Now you can see the whole beach with waves on one side and homes and streets on the other. Within a few more frames you are seeing the sun and the planets as little bitty specks against the larger backdrop of the galaxy. As you return, bit by bit to the beach you are aware of your unimportance, and at the same time your personal centrality to it all.

That's what's going in this book. The whole business of psychology, the whole point of view, the introspections of the clinical psychologists, the manipulations and deductions of the social psychologists, the endless animal extrapolations of the physiological psychologists, and even the social reforms of the radical psychologists are put into the full frame of human process.

One thing psychology lacks is a sense of history, not a nostalgic romantic, feet-by-the-fire sense of things past, but a functional awareness of the role that historical processes have in the development of psychological maturity and psychological pathology.

Nowhere in my training did we look at the effects of civilization on personal awareness. We looked endlessly at the individual life-style and life-cycle but never at the cultural life-cycle and never even envisioned the developmental cycle of the human species itself. History in my training usually meant something that happened about 10 to 20 years ago.

Psychologists will read this book and ask the litany of the behavioral scientists:

What is the experimental evidence?

What studies are referred to?

What experiments will make this prove out—true or false?

Alas and Alack (as they say in the sword and sorcery tales)

this volume does not meet any of those needs. It is not a psychology of. experiments and deductions from the results. It is a
discussion of a way to think, a way to examine the life-cycle. It
is a formulation of a more inclusive model of human functioning.

Warning—it is not a snappy, frothy book to read. It is written
for adults who are willing to follow a long and carefully drawn
argument from its inception to its conclusion.

Recently, I was at a symposium on consciousness, sponsored
by the California Institute of Transpersonal Psychology, with
Rudhyar. A number of super-stars of consciousness were present-
ing their most current work. Rudhyar spoke seldom but each
time he did the discussion shifted. Each time he would comment
or ask a question it would change the space we were thinking in.
He has the capacity to help others think in powers of ten, to rise
out of the internal bickerings over ideas to let both parties see
the nest in which their opposing ideas rest, like yin and yang
merged into one another. Some of the younger members of the
symposium didn't follow the thrust of his remarks and felt he
was taking them off the subject. They were right. He was asking
us to stop worrying our thoughts like a dog with a bone and
observe where our thinking arises and what its implications are.
I felt like a child being asked to grow up unexpectedly. The book
is like that.

I was in a supermarket line recently and ahead of me was a
man much, much older than I was. He was buying 10 pounds of
white sugar. Another man in line with us joked about the effects
of pure sugar as a diet for one so old. The man said, "I ain't old.
never have been, never will be. I'm 81 and I eat what I like."
In an instant he no longer was older; he was simply able to look
back farther than most people.

Rudhyar is 84 now and he isn't old either. He's mature enough
to take the time to say a thought fully, until it's finished; patient
enough to review its implications and compassionate enough to
write it out for others to see.

The first time I read this book, it was difficult for me to stay
with the argument, to maintain my attention. I saw that my
educational up-bringing has lessened my capacity to pay attention. The second time I read the book I could see how it has

begun to work on me, I was willing to walk along with Rudhyar and notice things as he pointed them out. My defensiveness had diminished, my pomposity about being a "real" psychologist had deflated. I realized I was in the presence of a great mind who was willing to clarify the place in which I found myself.

I suggest you read this book for pleasure, not for enlightenment (for you are already enlightened), not for scholarship, not for the sake of "keeping up," but to give yourself a larger set of windows to view your life from. It is a pleasure to know that books like this are still offered to us. It is a personal pleasure to commend it to you.

Though Rudhyar will probably snort at this I would suggest to you that he is in truth following an esoteric description from Alice Bailey (and hundreds of others who say it differently)

> The service that I render
>> must be to souls
>>> and not to myself . . .
> the fire that I create
>> must heat not burn:
>>> it must draw into its warmth
>>>> the man who needs its heat.*

—James Fadiman, Ph.D.
Stanford University,
California Institute of
Transpersonal Psychology

* Alice A. Bailey, *Discipleship in the New Age,* Vol. 1, p. 610.

Prologue

Synthesizing Mankind's Situation

1

A HOLISTIC APPROACH TO THE HUMAN SITUATION

In our age of compartmentalized knowledge and unrelated disciplines of thought, it is difficult for most minds to approach the human situation as a whole. This human situation is essentially twofold. A human being has to be considered both as an individual person and as a member of a collectivity.

Considered strictly as a biological and physical entity, a man not only belongs to the human species—a collectivity of organisms living in the Earth's biosphere—he also has many characteristics which differentiate him from any other human being. From a psychological and spiritual point of view, this man is a 'person' displaying a relatively autonomous character—a singular and self-defining way of acting and reacting, of feeling, thinking and making choices—and, to the extent that he does so, he (or she) can be said to be truly an 'individual'. Yet, however accentuated these differentiating traits may be, any individual is intimately related to the community within which he was born or is more or less permanently living. This state of relatedness does not refer merely to physical, organic and social activities; it has very deep and lasting, and in most cases ineradicable, features.

The life and personality of a human being can only be fully understood, and their characteristics defined, when considered not only from the point of view of *individual selfhood*, but also from that of *collective being*. A human being can and does operate in two ways. In some instances, he or she feels, thinks, and behaves as an individual; in others, as a member of a collectivity. He exists in two constantly interacting conditions. These can be separated only in intellectual analyses; in actual living they are not only inseparable, but interdependent. Like the *Yin* and the *Yang* of Chinese philosophy, these two conditions of human existence are polar opposites, yet they complement one another. If at any time and in a particular situation, one of the two is very strong, the other has to be weak. Yet even if one appears to dominate the field of consciousness and exclusively to dictate behavior, the other still operates in what the depth-psychologist calls the unconscious, ready to surge again into objective manifestation.

This dualism apparently is a fundamental feature of all modes of existence. The modern physicist discovers it at work in dealing with light. Paradoxically, light behaves in some situations as if made of "particles", in others, it propagates itself in the form of a "wave". If a human being is considered an individual self— or at a more metaphysical level, a "monad"—the particle-aspect of his existence is emphasized at the expense of the wave-aspect —that is, of his collective being. If for a time in a mob situation, a person feels, acts or thinks under the sway of mass emotions, what happens is that the collective aspect (or polarity) of his nature has forced the power of his individual selfhood to vanish; but, when the person has returned home, this power may once more emerge into the field of consciousness, and what was done as part of a mob is repudiated and perhaps even considered an episode of temporary insanity.

Modern psychologists are well aware of this existential dualism, and of the conscious and unconscious aspects of the human personality. Some psychologists approach the situation mainly from the point of view of individual selfhood; they deal with the problems arising from the fact that the individual self—and in most cases they mean the ego—tends often to be overwhelmed by the power of collective images and impulses. Some of these urges and impulses result from the release of biological stimulants such as hormones; others take a social and cultural character. When Carl Jung spoke of the collective unconscious, he should have differentiated between the *generic* unconscious based on biological energies, and the *socio-cultural* unconscious which refers to the innate dependence of an individual upon the great images and symbols of the culture, the family and religious tradition which molded the development of his mind when a child and adolescent. On the other hand, there are psychologists who emphasize the social factors in the consciousness of the human being and who tend to see a person as mainly the product of his environment and his culture.

The type of psychology which is mostly preoccupied with the development of the individual naturally considers the collective polarity in man as something to emerge from, thus as a psychic womb or a social matrix. The psychologist following such an approach in his therapy or counselling tends to give a negative meaning to the term "collective." He primarily associates it with unconsciousness and, even worse, with automatism and the identification of the consciousness with a traditional rigidly determining thinking, feeling and behavior. His task is to assist his client, confronted with the nearly inevitable crises met at various stages of "the process of individuation", to overcome the pull of his collective being. When experiencing these crises, the individual—or should we not rather say, the would-be individual—may feel so distraught, or at least so confused, that he tends to slide back and "return to the womb"—whether it be the psychically enfolding presence of his mother (or a substitute mother) or the collective matrix of cultural-social normality. How to deal with such a situation, or its indirect consequences, is the function of "individual psychology", which primarily means psychotherapy.

Can we, however, thoroughly and most meaningfully deal with this type of situation, so frequent in our period of human evolution, if we do not realize that what the human person on the path of psychological individualization experiences represents (or mirrors) in his brief personal life what humanity as a whole for many centuries has been experiencing, is still now experiencing, and undoubtedly will experience for millennia to come? The individual's crises, his helplessness when strong biological urges seize his consciousness, his frequent relapses into subservience to the unquestioned collective paradigms of his culture, his inability to stand as an individual in a mass-situation and his refusal to bow to the dictates of "fashion" in whatever field of activity it may be, all these reflect the crises, the periodic collapses and disintegration mankind has been experiencing during the few millennia of recorded history. The character of the *collective factor* operating in any human being is conditioned by that of the state of evolution of mankind at the time this person lives. This collective factor is in evidence in the primordial condition of living of human beings. Mankind is prior to individual men and women. Individuals emerge out of collective states of being —an often forgotten fact.

Human evolution is a tide that breaks into billions of small wavelets, cresting and troughing. Each wavelet is potentially an individual person. The condition of the shore on which the tide breaks, plus the influence of the wind and of deep oceanic currents, produce an immense variety of *human situations,* each of which may emerge as an autonomous person with a strongly individualized and unique consciousness of self and individual purpose. As these individualizing wavelets crest, we observe a human being beginning to think, feel, act and respond to life's challenges as an individual.

This symbolical analogy must evidently not be taken too literally; yet it can be revealing if we add that as the planetary tide of human evolution breaks upon the shore, the individualizing wavelet ceases to operate according to its wave nature. It acts as a "particle"—that is as a relatively independent entity —a living organism. As an animal this organism enters a new field of existential activity. In this field it would soon be destroyed by other entities or forces of nature, if it did not unite with other individuals in order to more securely and effectively meet the challenges of a new and totally unfamiliar life-situation. Uniting with other individuals means forming a group; and at that level of mankind, a collective consciousness emerges within the group, resulting from communal behavior, memories and expectations. As this happens, the collective factor in human nature finds itself re-energized; but it now operates within a socio-cultural frame of reference. This transformation occurs in the animal kingdom, but it reaches a most extensive stage at the human level of planetary evolution. It also becomes the foundation upon which a further evolutionary state of existence develops. The socio-cultural collectivity that almost totally controls the consciousness and the activities of human persons at the tribal and even post-tribal stage becomes the matrix out of which conscious and relatively autonomous individuals emerge. The individual polarity of human nature thus reasserts itself powerfully, and often destructively. Individualized men and women develop an acute feeling of separateness, and even alienation and isolation, which generates the many tensions, problems and traumas with which psychologists have to deal.

However individualized and separate modern men and women may be, the basic, yet almost totally forgotten fact is that their physical organisms, from which all forms of activities and all types of consciousness are primordially derived, are constituted mainly by *sea water*. It is the same kind of sea water, however different the races, cultures and personalities. The original oceanic state remains the foundation of life in every living organism, be it the body of the greatest genius, saint or 'perfect Master'. It is the primordial stuff out of which the *generic* unconscious develops. One might call it the foundation of the planetary life serving as a substratum for the process of generic differentiation of Earth-life into a multitude of animal species, with *homo sapiens* as the present apex of the differentiating biological evolution.

At the oceanic sea-water stage, the One Life of the planet seems to be the only reality; but it moves to and fro in tidal activity. At the stage of animal existence, while there are many physically separate organisms, the individual specimens are only very slight variations on the one theme of the species. The generic collective factor almost totally dominates; yet the individual factor can already be seen on the rise. In primitive tribal mankind, a new element begins to operate the moment man gives a symbolic form to group-togetherness. Tribesmen not only actively cooperate in order to satisfy biological needs, they communicate in order to cooperate more effectively. They develop the ability to refer their experiences to a center and thus to give them a conscious meaning and purpose. At first this center is felt to exist outside of the physical organism. The whole tribe has a center and this center is deified, sacrificed to, and worshipped. The ability to survive, better cope with, and enjoy the experiences of human existence inherent in collective living is given an individual character. The tribe thus becomes a *collective person*.

As tribes expand and interrelate, the ever-increasing complexity of interpersonal and intercommunal relationships calls for a centralized form of organization. It takes the form of a kingdom ruled from a large city where an all-powerful king is enthroned. This king becomes thus the embodied manifestation —or collective psychological 'projection'—of the principle of unity at the socio-cultural level of human activity and consciousness. He is at first worshipped as a god; later on, he is said to rule by divine right. Institutionalized religion sanctions his power, forcing the people to accept transcendental but rigid patterns of collective thinking and feeling.

The king, who at first was the wholesome embodiment of the ability to deal with neighboring tribes or nations and the holistic symbol of the centralized power of a national community, turns into a tyrannical force operating arbitrarily and arrogantly, and uses a formalistic and tentacular bureaucracy to bolster his control. A time comes when the power of the individual polarity in human nature must reassert itself in the rebellion of a few visionary and creative persons. Eventually the realization that every human being potentially has his own center, not only in terms of organic bio-social activity, but in terms of a vivid, deep, incontrovertible realization of individual selfhood and spiritual autonomy, leads to the Hindu ideal of spiritual 'liberation' and the Western concept of democracy and political freedom. Because spiritual liberation is not easily reached at our stage of human evolution, political liberty is sought as a material substitute.

Whether a human being strives first and foremost for spiritual liberation or for the political freedom associated with a type of society extolling—as a basic principle—the right to be and act as an individual, personal problems are bound to arise at the psychological level. India has her madmen whose psychic integrity collapsed during the crises of transformation on the path to liberation. The Western world, and particularly our American nation, contains an ever-increasing number of acute neurotics and psychotics in whom the tensions generated by the dialectic process of individualization out of the collective socio-cultural womb turned destructive of personal integration.

The approach a particular culture takes in dealing with psychological crises and the disintegrative consequences of the at least partial inability to meet them constructively and/or transformatively is always based on a set of implicit assumptions concerning man and his development. Hindu psychology is very often descriptive, listing a great number of emotions or psychic attitudes and their opposites; yet its seemingly empirical and experiential approach is firmly rooted in metaphysical concepts and assumptions on which the whole Hindu culture with its various branches is based. Euro-American psychology, which for a long time was the handmaid of theology and the servant of a religio-social type of morality intertwined with intellectual rationalism, has now accepted wholesale the empiricism and statistical methods of modern science.

The Western approach depends on the objective observation and study of an at least relatively vast number of particular cases, and on statistical generalizations derived from the raw data produced by research and experiments. Out of the correlation, classification and evaluation of 'significant' data, the psychologist hopes to see structural patterns emerging. These patterns guide him in assessing the character of psychological events, providing effective solutions to emotional problems, and dissolving complexes whose gyroscopic rigidity block the flow of 'psychic energy' (libido). Each school of psychology generates a more or less specific type of psychotherapy, analytical or integrative, meditational or actional, rationalistic or experiential.

No attempt will be made in this book to produce a new model for psychotherapy. The field is already saturated, and Dr. Assagioli's 'Psychosynthesis' presents the theoretical possibility of including any and all systems of therapy. What I am trying to do in this volume is to eludicate the nature of *the human situation* which forms the background of all psychological enquiries and analyses. It is to present a *structural* rather than empirical type of psychology, in which the collective planet-wide development of mankind as a whole provides an intensely significant,

and indeed compelling background for the tension-generating
and crisis-stimulating process of individualization out of various
types of social 'wombs', and—in the Jungian sense—of person-
ality-integration and individuation.

Such a type of structural psychology unavoidably rests upon
a metaphysical foundation, but actually, *every* kind of psychology implies a more or less clearly formulated philosophy, a
particular *Weltanschauung* (world view). The psychologist usually does not question the validity of that philosophy, because
it is sanctioned by the socio-cultural Establishment or by an
age-old tradition. For instance, the empiricism which characterizes the scientific mentality of the Western world is based on a
set of assumptions regarding knowledge and the validity of data
and their statistical treatment. These assumptions can be considered 'true' in the limited field defined by man's *present* sense-
perceptions and the nature of the rationalistic processes characterizing the intellect (as we now understand this term); but,
they certainly cannot be called absolutely true. They need not
be considered valid for a consciousness that would operate in
space-time conditions radically different from those found in the
Earth's biosphere. The most progressive 'philosophers of science'
of our day are aware of this,[1] but the mentality of the majority
of scientists, school teachers, and psychologists has not yet been
deeply affected by the new realities of atomic and nuclear
physics.

The metaphysical concepts underlying a structural psychology
such as this book presents can be very simply expressed because
they are derived from a generalization of the most basic human
experience, the experience of change. What is assumed is that
change, and therefore some kind of motion, are unceasing and
present everywhere. Moreover, when we speak of 'existence'
we refer to processes of change occurring within finite 'fields'
during equally finite time-spans. We also know that energy is
released discontinuously in *quanta* (packages of energy). As it is

---

[1] Cf. particularly, a remarkable recent book by Fritjof Capra, *The Tao
of Physics* (Berkeley: Shambhala Publications, 1975) and a French work
by Robert Linssen, *La Spiritualité de la Matière* (Paris: Editions Planète,
1966).

released, it produces its own field. Within that field, definite types of *activity* take place. We speak of activity when motion (i.e., dynamic energy) and the changes it produces occur within a field or in the relationship between two or more fields.

Activity so understood does not necessarily imply an 'actor'. The concept of actor arises in our mind only when we realize that a particular kind of field of activity has a center which to some extent controls or guides, and in some manner is aware of the resulting changes. The degree of control and the quality of the awareness vary enormously. Yet the belief that some type of consciousness, however rudimentary and imprecise, exists in every centralized field of activity is gradually being accepted by the vanguard of Western thinkers. It has pervaded most ancient philosophies and the instinctual approach to existence of all archaic people. Consciousness and field-activity are inseparable.

A finite field of activity constitutes a whole. As Jan Smuts pointed out in his most important and seminal work, *Holism and Evolution* (London: Macmillan, 1926), our universe is a universe of wholes. Human experience deals with wholes and with the results of the interaction of wholes or of the disintegration of larger wholes into smaller ones. Moreover, man witnesses a hierarchy of wholes everywhere—any whole having parts which themselves are wholes having parts. Smuts considered evolution a drive toward more inclusive wholeness—calling such a drive, *holism*.[2] Unfortunately, the limiting field of his Western tradition and mentality made it seemingly impossible for him to envision a more inclusive whole than what he called "personality", and possibly a more primary whole than the atom. Neither did he seem to have as clear a concept of the inseparability of the state of existential wholeness and of consciousness as for instance his contemporary, Teilhard de Chardin.

---

[2] The contrast between the 'holistic' and 'atomistic' approach to knowledge and reality has been discussed by a few modern thinkers, particularly by Lancelot L. Whyte in his significant book, *Accent on Form* (New York: Harper, 1954), pp. 46-68. Yet while the adjective, holistic, is now currently in use in science, philosophy and psychology, Jan Smuts' book is hardly ever mentioned. The words, holism and holistic, (from the Greek *olos*, meaning 'whole') may have been used before General Smuts used them, but it certainly was his book which introduced them to a wide public.

In the philosophy I have presented, the principle of wholeness directly and inevitably manifests as consciousness.[3] Wherever there are finite fields of activity, there is consciousness. The atom is conscious, and so is the cosmos because the cosmos is a finite field of activity, a whole. Somewhere in between these two field-magnitudes—perhaps exactly at the mid-point—stands the human being, who is also finite and conscious. Only infinity —if we can really conceive of such a condition—would be unconscious.

Indian philosophy, particularly as reformulated by Sri Aurobindo, speaks of the two aspects of Brahman—manifest and unmanifest.[4] In his manifested aspect, Brahman is the Unity-aspect of the cosmos, *Ishvara*. In our Christian Western tradition, this original and originating One is called God—the Creator or the Logos who manifests in the world as a divine Trinity. The great Christian mystic, Meister Eckart, nevertheless introduced the utterly transcendent concept of "the Godhead" that corresponds to the unmanifested Brahman, also spoken of as Tat, and in China, Tao. All these terms refer to what must be considered ineffable, infinite, timeless, spaceless, changeless, and, we must add, 'unconscious'. Yet by so doing, we are merely accumulating meaningless negatives—various ways of denying the character of existential reality to that which is both being and non-being and transcends all dualities, including the contrast between unity and multiplicity, or spirit and matter. It seems that the most meaningful concept we can make is that of absolute or infinite *potentiality*. We can also figuratively speak of an 'Ocean of potential energy'; but *energy simply means the potentiality of activity*.

The most realistic idea we can have of the *manifested* aspect of Brahman is that of 'existences'. Existence includes *activity* and *form* (the principle of rhythm in time and finiteness in space). Activity within the structural limitation of form reso-

[3] Cf. my *The Planetarization of Consciousness* (New York: A. S. I. Publications, second edition, 1977), p. 111, "Consciousness, Wholeness and Relatedness."

[4] Cf. his beautiful *Commentaries on the Isha Upanished* (Arya Publishing House, 1914).

nates as *consciousness*. This trinity of principles may be said to correspond to the Hindu trinity of *Sat-Chit-Ananda*. While this is usually translated as Being-Consciousness-Bliss, a more basic translation may be: *Sat*, activity; *Chit*, the principle of form, which implies relatedness; *Ananda*, consciousness, which when fulfilled and all-inclusive (i.e., holistic) produces a state of 'illumination' or 'bliss'.

A whole having a relatively permanent and existential character is structured; the term, structure, meaning here an internal arrangement and organization of parts. In any *natural* whole—any 'existent'—the relationship between these parts is dynamic and constantly changing. Within the existential whole—a finite field of potential as well as kinetic energy—activity differentiates into functions. Functions are categories of activity referred to the whole and serving its purpose—its *dharma* or 'fundamental nature'. All functions within the activity field are interrelated and interdependent. Moreover, there are several levels of functioning. Four such levels can be distinguished; some functions link one level to the next. We shall call them 'functions of transition' or 'seed functions'.

At the biological level of organization, where human beings operate as physical bodies, activity in its unitary aspect is called 'life' or the life-force—known as *prana* in India, *chi* in China, and by different names in different cultures at different epochs. The living organism in animals and human beings maintains itself and transforms and reproduces itself through the operation of some basic functions: nerve-communication, blood circulation, respiration, digestion, sense-perception, muscular response, memory, sex, and perhaps a power of transformation or mutation linked with sex—possibly the Hindu *Kundalini*.

Human beings do not act merely at the biological level; they also operate as *social* beings belonging to fields of activity within which a large number of human bodies are interrelated within a limited geographical space. These fields are called 'societies'; they are structured along quite definite lines by institutionalized processes and laws. These societies are therefore 'wholes' of a particular type. They use energy; they display collective rhythms, and they have a more or less definite span of existence.

At a certain stage of human evolution men or women, reacting in different ways to the pressures exerted by the social organism in which they perform (or fail to perform) various roles, develop a set of feeling-responses and a type of consciousness which bring them to a new state of relationship with their society and its tradition. They feel separate, isolated from the social community. They aspire to become, and strive to operate as independent persons—self-reliant and self-motivated. They try to actualize their own individual potentialities of action and consciousness in terms of an ideal of integral fulfillment and perfection.

This does not mean that these individuals (or would-be individuals) cease to operate at the biological level of activity; they obviously remain conditioned by their body-functions, their life-instincts, and some basic biopsychic drives. Neither do they necessarily break their contact with their social community, though some may do so in a more or less overt and radical manner; for instance, there is the Hindu yogi who leaves family and village to meditate for long years in a Himalayan cave. But the relationship of these autonomy-seekers to both their biopsychic organism and their social collectivity takes on a profoundly different character. In them the *individual* pole of human nature stands in conscious and determined polar opposition to the *generic-collective* polarity; and opposition not only produces conflicts, it also induces a state of spiritual isolation and, perhaps, a tragic sense of alienation. The conflict-situation breeds aggressiveness and, in many cases, violence. If outwardly and inwardly unsuccessful their drive toward a radical and absolute kind of individualism often leads to acute depression and various modes of escape, from drug addition to psychosis.

Whether successful or unsuccessful, the individualizing process has a particularly dynamic character. It forces a constant, or at least a periodic, facing of issues because however much a person may emphasize the individual pole of human nature, he or she remains, in an almost inescapable way, 'biologically human'. "Man's common humanity" (I used this phrase in my small book, *The Faith that Gives Meaning to Victory;* New York, 1942), is the root-foundation of 'personality'—the human flower. The state of society refers to the plant's green leaves.

Beyond roots, leaves, and flowers, and constituting the alpha and omega of the plant's cycle of existence, we find the seed. With this symbolical seed we reach a fourth level or 'order' of functions. At this level, transcendental processes of activity and consciousness operate. In our Western civilization, we still know very little concerning the nature of these processes, but in Hindu philosophy and yoga or what generally may be called the 'esoteric Tradition', this fourth level of activity is dealt with extensively. In a sense, it is a *human* level but it could be more significantly called *trans*-human. It is also trans-*social*. For it to achieve human manifestation, the prior development of a culture and its "Prime Symbols" (Spengler) as a psychomental foundation is required. It is also *transpersonal* because the functions of the fourth order operate *through* the personality and *across* its psychic boundaries. They relate in individual persons in terms of a fourth dimension whose keynote is INTERPENETRATION.

A holistic structural psychology has to deal with all the four levels of activity at which human beings can, but usually do not, operate. It has to understand the character of the most basic functions in which, at each level, human activity is differentiated, as human beings proceed in their long multimillennial evolution on this planet, Earth, in which mankind operates as a functional system of activity. It has to recognize the critical nature of certain functions which, though belonging originally to one level, serve as agencies to induce or catalyze the development of the next higher level. For example, we shall see that, though at first the manifestation of a purely biological need, sexual activity serves as a starting point for the development of social processes and culture. A certain kind of mental activity likewise makes possible a shift from the second order of functions (social level) to the third order (personal-individual level).

In the next two chapters, the four orders of function and the functions of transition will be discussed. In so doing, I shall concern myself almost solely with the operation of some of the most basic among these functions in the lives of human beings considered as single persons. Thus I shall approach the human situation from the point of view of the individual polarity of human existence. This is the approach we generally associate with psychology—particularly 'individual psychology' and 'humanistic psychology', or, I might say, *person-centered* psychology.

Psychotherapy is more or less inevitably based on such an approach, because it deals with the problems and mental illnesses of individuals. Yet no individual is ill in a vacuum. *All* individual disturbances occur in the context of the evolution of humanity as a whole. Socio-cultural conflicts and pressures—including those experienced within a modern type of 'nuclear' (or atomistic) family—form the background of *any* personal disturbance, whether its symptoms are psychological or biological; and they are usually both. It is, therefore, imperative for the psychologist to become clearly aware of the stage in its evolution at which mankind as a whole stands today. Yet, few psychologists have a clear understanding of history. This is not entirely their fault because, throughout their education from elementary grades through college, history has been presented to them in a piecemeal, fragmented, events-oriented, un-holistic manner. Interesting as the collected data may be, they do not provide a deeply human understanding of the overall evolutionary meaning of the present world-crisis affecting all human beings and even all kingdoms of nature. Sensitive people are ill, and disturbed persons become psychotic, *in relation to* this world-crisis.

One can endlessly argue whether the individual or society comes first. At the level of physical manifestation, an individual person is born within, and emerges out of, a society whose collective values mold his or her behavior and consciousness. Society comes first—not the individual. The individual can be said to be prior to society (the collective factor) only if we assume the pre-existence of a soul (or monad) in a transcendent realm of being. But it is questionable whether the concept of essentially separate monads or spiritual Soul-centers is absolutely valid, regardless of what Leibnitz and the philosophers of the personalistic school assert, and what a *popular* approach to spirituality and occultism usually makes us believe. Nevertheless it is relatively valid and, therefore, have been emphasized even by 'spiritual Teachers', because humanity is at the stage at which the main *need* of mankind has been to complete and make more thorough and radical the process of individualization—the emergence of individuals out of the womb of *physical nature*, the collective Earth-mother.

Unfortunately, the evolutionary drive toward individualization has led in many places, especially in the Western world, to a disharmonic over-emphasis of individualism—a violently egocentric and exclusivistic kind of 'rugged individualism'. One polarity of human nature has been stressed *against* the other; and there can be no wholesome development where the 'against' attitude prevails, legitimate as it seems to be at first. What is required is a *counterpoint* type of growth. The newly developing faculty should find its expression in the upper melodic line which gives its essential meaning to the whole; yet the line forming the bass voice is also significant. At a further stage of development, a still higher line of unfoldment appears which takes as its basis the combined values of bass and tenor. That higher (which really means 'more inclusive') manifestation presents itself to man's consciousness as a melody of colored light.

The entire process of human evolution has a dialectical character. To the *thesis*, represented by the tribal stage of relatively unconscious (because compulsive and instinctual) collective existence, succeeds the antithetic phase of individualization. *Antithesis* produces conflicts, because the drive toward individual and group differentiation requires the formation of an *élite* (an aristocracy) along whatever line of development is *needed* at the time. Conflicts engender crises; and, out of crises successfully met and *lived through*, a new level of consciousness and a more inclusive type of feeling and behaving is reached. It is reached, at first, by a very few human beings. In some of them, unfortunately, the newly released awareness and energy are captured by an as yet unpurified ego; other individuals accept to become truly 'servants' of a 'higher' superpersonal collectivity. In these 'servants', *through* them, the discordant Babel of individual voices becomes transmuted into the cosmic collectivism of what we symbolically call 'light', or in another sense, the true fourth dimension of being and consciousness which manifests as harmonic interpenetration and radiant co-activity.

This cyclic historical or evolutionary process will be briefly discussed in the second part of this book. It must be discussed if psychologists are to meet, with inclusive understanding and creative lucidity, the problems forcing themselves upon the men and women of our time. These problems, and the excruciating tensions they produce, cannot be approached with full satisfaction by merely collating empirical data and from them making statistical generalizations and intellectual theories along strictly psychological lines. Our modern Western culture is sick with fragmentation and specialization. Techniques alone can never go to the roots of any human issue. The interpenetration of individualized consciousness alone can change the quality of human relationships, and, therefore, gradually the quality of social processes.

This is why Oriental cultures stress the need for a guru-chela relationship. Not primarily for the purpose of conveying knowledge, but in order to allow two minds to interpenetrate, making it possible for the narrower and more rigid field of activity and consciousness to resonate to the wider, more open and more inclusive one. True education is co-penetration and fecundation of minds. Spiritual living implies openness of the dis-egoized individual consciousness to the radiance and the 'gift-waves' of a higher collectivity. It is transpersonal living—a focusing of diffuse collective light through the lens of an individual, yet translucent, mind.

As a result of such a focusing, activity reaches a point of transforming creative intensity. Whether the spiritual-mental heat thus generated will warm and inspire those who surround the focalized radiance, or produce in them ego-withdrawal and emotional insecurity, depends not only upon the character of the persons being touched, but of the state of the neighboring collectivity—thus of the timing and place of the release. For this reason, the effectiveness of psychotherapy, as well of any spiritual teaching, should not be considered only an individual matter. The whole of humanity is involved in the responses of every individual.

Part One

The Personal-Individual Mode

2

THE FOUR ORDERS OF FUNCTION

a. *Functions of the First Order*

The first order of functions can be called biological because they operate, in one form or another, in all living organisms within the Earth's biosphere. Among these functions we shall simply mention (a) breathing; (b) the circulation of vitalizing and reparative fluids (whether they be sap, blood, lymph or cerebro-spinal fluid); (c) the electro-chemical operation of nerve-transmission; (d) the production of hormones and antibodies by glands or nodules of various kinds; (e) the complex process of digestion, metabolism, and waste-elimination; (f) the capacity of muscle tissues to contract and relax; and (g) the many-sided operations related to growth and maturity. I should also mention the process of sleep and dreaming, for except in extra-ordinary cases, this process is necessary for survival.

Sexual activity is a biological function; yet, especially in human beings, it occupies a specific position in the fundamental hierarchy. We will presently deal with sex as a function of transition—or seed, function—which, though in its primary mode of activity and biological purpose belongs to the first order, also becomes the foundation for processes referring to the second order of functions. These, once developed, produce the multifarious activities of the socio-cultural level of human existence.

Functions of the first order are 'generic', in the sense that they are common to or shared by all human beings; they differ somewhat, but not fundamentally, from race to race, and even less from person to person. If to some extent repressed or impaired (permanently or for a relatively long time) these functions produce definite psychosomatic disturbances. Most of these functional and periodic activities are necessary for survival. They have a definite rhythm. They are direct differentiations of the

21

basic life-force, called by as many names as there are cultures and subcultural schools of thought.

These functions are essentially compulsive, instinctual, automatic and repetitive. They are unconscious, taken for granted and normally not directly subject to what we call the *will*, though some, and perhaps at a certain stage of human development, all of them may be controlled by an individual's mind and will operating as a function of the third order. Biological functions have psychic 'overtones', even at the primary level of human evolution; but these overtones are rooted in and entirely dependent upon the operation of the biological functions. They reflect the wholesome or impaired nature of the instrumentalities (cells and organic structures) through which the related functions operate.

A time comes, however, when what was at first a more or less evanescent overtone—an uncertain and easily dissipated 'resonance' affecting the inner life of a human being—can reach such a state of critical intensity that it seems to act as a 'fundamental tone' carrying the main life-accent. As the consciousness and will of a particular human being in a particular life-situation focus themselves upon a new type of function—a function of the second (and eventually third) order—a transfer of energy occurs which depotentializes the function of the first order constituting its infrastructure. This depotentialization may be temporary or, on the other hand relatively permanent. It may represent a progressive condition of human growth, or lead to a regressive state and the kind of ill-health to which the whole person is not able to give a constructive meaning and purpose. Yet, there are illnesses or operational defects at the biological level to which a highly constructive and metamorphic meaning *can* be given by an individual able to interpret them from a life-transcendent (metabiological) point of view.

b. *Functions of the Second Order*

Existence is based on relatedness. Life cannot exist without some kind of relationship. All the basic biological functions imply specific forms of relationship in which a living organism either absorbs various inorganic substances (air, water, minerals) or eats and assimilates other living organisms and their products (for instance, fruits and seeds). Eating is a fundamental biological need. The law of the biosphere is: Eat or be eaten. Hunger is a relentless drive related to the 'nutritive function'. The need for security produces another kind of drive based on the operation of the function of organic preservation and self-maintenance which especially manifests as the capacity to defend oneself against other organisms or natural forces.

These three functions of the first order imply relationship with other organisms. Eating means being related in a special manner with what is being eaten. Sexual activity, at the instinctual and natural level, requires a partner of opposite biological polarity. Security at the jungle state of existence in most instances demands the *co*-operation of several living organisms, according to the adage, "In union there is strength."

At the strictly biological level of activity, the living organism *uses* relationship to fulfill what its functional activities need in order to operate as well as possible; but when the factor of relatedness is given a significance and value that in some manner imbues the activity with a character transcending the strictly biological need, functions of the second order can be said to appear. They display a new *operational quality* and therefore produce (or induce) a new type of consciousness—social consciousness.

Social consciousness evidently exists at the animal level; yet it most likely does not reach the stage of autonomous development until the activities of human beings, living in rather clearly defined and relatively permanent groups, become differentiated —some human beings becoming specialists in a particular field of activity, others in another field. The most basic differentiation is at first purely biological, being the inevitable result of differences between male and female types of sexual and procreative activity. It implies also the difference between children and adults, a difference which in tribal groups, to some extent at least, is eradicated by the sacred rites of puberty. As the evolution of tribal societies proceeds, clans or specialized groups develop, each being charged with the responsibility of satisfying a particular functional need of the society-as-a-whole. This eventually leads to the establishment of castes and social classes.*

The important point is, that at first the formation of differentiated groups of human beings within a tribal collectivity is purely a projection of the biological functions upon a but rudimentary and undeveloped layer of consciousness. Biological functions operate in a condition we today call 'unconsciousness', even though a subhuman kind of consciousness should be attributed to cells and perhaps to the physical-body-as-a-whole (we speak now, at least figuratively, of the "wisdom of the body"). Consciousness, in the present-day ordinary sense of the term, develops with social processes, because it is based on the emergence and the progressive ascendancy of the *sense of relatedness,* gradually detaching itself from its biological base.

As human beings in tribal groups begin to *cultivate* this sense of togetherness and relatedness, above and beyond the fulfillment of strictly biological needs, social functions develop which seek to give to the fact of group-relationship a *collective meaning.* This meaning in turn, by increasing the cohesion of the group, makes the group activity more efficacious. But this increase in effectiveness is presented as subservient to a 'higher' realization, that of the 'unity' of the group. At least it is so presented by a special kind of human beings—medicine-men, seers, high priests, and later, philosophers—whose *social* function it is to give to this sense of *unity in relatedness* a religious and cultural formulation. The newly developed social function is glorified and projected as an existential—even though supernal and mysterious—reality, the god of the tribe. It finds its actional and concretized manifestation in rituals, myths and symbols, and thus a particular culture is born.

Functions of the second order are socio-cultural, and the most basic of them answers the need for *communication.* This need is met by the development of various types of language. There is a language of gestures, a language using relatively isolated

---

* Such a functional differentiation is very marked in the societies of ants and bees, but the extent to which it affects the consciousness of the units in the differentiated groups is unknown.

onomatopoeic vocal sounds to evoke collective experiences, and a language describing and defining actional processes through verbs, nouns, qualificatives suggesting existential qualities, and connective terms referring to the relation between all the various factors.

These forms of communication develop, on the one hand, into symbolic art-forms evoking intangible, subjective feelings or realizations rather than describing the interaction of physical entities, and on the other hand, into various systematized forms of mental activities. These essentially have the character of 'revelation'. Life, or the god who controls all the life processes, reveals to the more sensitive human organisms whatever knowledge they need, not only to physically survive, but to bring to the fullest possible development a particular quality of human existence, activity and consciousness characterizing the communal group to which it is addressed.

From language and various forms of revealed types of activity presented as unbreakable taboos or divine commandments, socio-cultural institutions develop which further concretize and crystallize the sense of relatedness and tribal (later social) interdependence. These institutions increasingly bind together, and mentally as well as emotionally integrate, the participants into a collective *culture-whole*. A culture-whole can be considered a socio-cultural organism in the sense that it is an organized system (or field) of interrelated and interdependent human activities, integrated by a deep-seated feeling of community and a commonness of traditions and basic purpose. Culture-wholes are originally most closely related to, and even identified with, a clearly defined geographical territory, a particular climate, a special fauna and flora, and resources of various kinds. The culture-whole is 'rooted' in the biosphere and to this extent it is based on functions of the first order which give it a solidity— the solidity of rootedness. But, as already stated, if biology is the root, the socio-cultural activity represents the foliage. The tree of human collectivity eventually blossoms forth into individual persons.

Culture does not deny biology; it differentiates and refines biological activity, reorienting and controlling it, so as to stabilize and extend it. This makes far more complex and, above all, more consciously meaningful, the interaction and interdependence of the many members of a social organism; and this, not only within a spatial field, but throughout the entire life-span of that organism, the span of many centuries. Here we come to what differentiates human from animal societies. A human society is not merely concerned with the satisfaction of a collective need for security and steady growth; it also is intent on developing conditions of living and a state of consciousness allowing for the peaceful transfer of information, knowledge, meaning, and purpose from generation to generation. The value of such a transfer of culture parallels, at a non-physical level, the importance of genetic selection and of producing relatively stable lines of genetic development at the biological level. To use a significant phrase coined more than fifty years ago by Count Alfred Korzybski in his early book, *The Manhood of Humanity*, man has a "time-binding" capacity—while animals, thanks to their ability for locomotion, 'bind space', and plants 'bind chemical elements', particularly in photosynthesis.

The time-binding capacity implies the ability to produce symbols which not only carry concrete and eventually technical information in the form of words and glyphs or diagrams of various types, but may also convey meaning and a quality of understanding, from which wisdom can emerge as a guiding force for future generations. At first, symbols are almost entirely based on the common biological, seasonal and agricultural experience of the human beings belonging to a particular culture-whole (or society), but they gradually assume an abstract character, referring no longer as much to the character and behavior of physical entities and forces of nature as to *the relationship* between entities or the acts they perform. These relationships produce not only physically observable results, but also subjective feelings—whether in individual persons or in large groups.

Knowledge born of accumulated observations and experiments, and of the classification and generalization of these data, leads to the growth of a mental attitude which is not only objective, but at least potentially transformative. *Wisdom*, likewise, can act as a transformative force, for events—whether present, expected, or past—can be transformed by the meaning given to them. Such transformations raise the consciousness to a higher vibratory pitch. The circularity and repetitiveness of biological instincts becomes, as a result, the spiral of conscious human evolution.

The question of whether animals have 'intelligence' or only 'instincts' is perhaps more semantic than realistic, though the great French philosopher, Henri Bergson, whose ideas had a tremendous influence during the first part of our century, stressed what to him was a basic difference between the two words. Yet, not only in animals, but as well in primitive man, mind operates exclusively at the service of the biological needs for survival, security and food. 'Life' totally controls 'mind'. Mind, however, can free itself from such a control, because mind is simply consciousness in a formed (or structured) state. It is *consciousness stabilized and defined at a particular level of activity*. When the level of activity of an existential whole—and therefore of the consciousness associated with this activity—changes, the mind, which is a part of this whole, becomes transformed.

As already stated and more extensively formulated in my book *The Planetarization of Consciousness*, consciousness is simply another aspect of wholeness. The existence of an existential whole implies a particular inner organization of its parts or components; and this organization, in turn, implies some degree of consciousness. Every existential whole is in a process of change. It is both internally and externally active. Activity implies an expenditure of potential energy. Thus, all these terms—activity, energy, wholeness, organization, and consciousness—are interdependent aspects of the same reality; i.e., of the complex, rhythmic, and ordered process we call existence. What has to be considered is *the level* at which the existential process operates. Difference of level of activity implies difference of vibratory frequency (in terms of energy release) and difference in the character and scope, the quality and inclusiveness of the consciousness.

Thus, when the human organism operates almost exclusively at the level of 'life', its consciousness has the character and quality of biological activity and biological functions. Life, in the strict sense of biological activity on the Earth's surface, operates in terms of *physicality*, that is, it deals with and organizes materials which have a great deal of mass and inertia. Life at the level of the vegetable and animal kingdoms manifests in and through material bodies constituting organized fields of essentially physical activity, with a low rate of vibratory frequency and a great deal of resistance to change and 'acceleration' or intensification. But at the human level, while life's operation is still basically conditioned by the physicality of the human body, a new and 'higher' potentiality begins to operate.

This potentiality of rhythmic transformation and intensification of consciousness at first operates in a most tentative and imprecisely focused manner; it is constantly overwhelmed by the powerful rhythms and demands of the biological functions. Yet it is inherent in *any* human organism. By its very presence, it acts in a deep subconscious manner at the core of every human organism; and the essential function of 'culture' (in the highest and most human sense of the word) is to *cradle* the actualization of this new potentiality.

If used in its broadest meaning, the term 'society' applies to the level of animal as well as human activity; but at the animal level, society is totally dominated by the physicality of biological functions. As humanity gradually and more clearly defines its 'humanness' and raises the focus of its collective consciousness to an ever-higher level, human societies gradually respond to the vibration of a new level of existential activity. Cultural activities and institutions which at first were still entirely pervaded with biological motivation, progressively—yet hesitantly —attempt to incorporate qualities belonging to a transphysical level of consciousness. Culture becomes impregnated with what I have defined as the process of 'civilization'. I use this word in its most inclusive sense, a sense which accounts for its present negative and catabolic aspect in our megalopoles; but it also includes the ideal aspect symbolized in esoteric tradition by the "Holy City", *Hieros Salem* (the sacred place of Peace), or the future Shambhala that stands in relation to the ancient Shambhala as the Omega to the Alpha state of *human* evolution.[1]

[1] For a full discussion of the concepts of culture and civilization, *see* my book, *Culture, Crisis and Creativity* (Wheaton: Theosophical Publishing House, 1977).

Human culture takes on a more strictly 'human' character when the symbols it creates are interrelated to constitute an ever more abstract, and therefore less physically concrete (and even less biologically conditioned), type of 'language'; this is the language of modern science, thanks to whose information technology has developed with intensely transformative results. In a sense, this is the language of 'civilization', and it finds its ultimate expression in mathematics, with its group-algebra and its ever more rarefied concepts of multidimensions and time-reversal which seek to transcend the most basic experiences of human existence, that of directional change. The use of mathematics in the interpretation of indirectly observed sub-atomic phenomena has led to a transphysical and superrational relativistic picture of the universe.

As Fritjof Capra points out in his already-mentioned book, *The Tao of Physics,* such a picture is strikingly similar to those which Oriental and Western mystics and seers have sought to evoke through the use of paradoxes intending to challenge and confuse or break down the mind bound to concrete phenomena and rationalistic sequences. Erotic symbols have also frequently been used to draw the too-personalized consciousness to the rare life-moments when the everyday sense of ego-separateness is most likely to be swept away by a unifying tide of emotional intensity.

What this means is that the development of culture may have to take different forms in different places in order to produce essentially similar results. The ultimate aim of human evolution is the raising of the focus of consciousness and, as a result (or at the same time), the freeing of human activity from its bondage to physicality and biology by providing for it new channels of expression. If modern science, mathematics, and the transcendent vistas of atomic physics and intergalactic astronomy have today come to occupy a place of dominant influence in a world largely controlled by our Western type of mentality, it is because this influence was needed to cope with the rapid development, especially in Europe and America, of the new functions of the *third* order related to the process of individualization.

Since the sixth century B. C., and especially since the European Renaissance, this process has accelerated to such an extent that it has given rise to critical social and cultural tensions and conflicts, and to endless personal problems. These social conflicts and psychological problems have to be faced with a holistic type of understanding; and I believe that such an understanding can best be gained when the elements of our present world-crisis are approached and evaluated in terms of the sequential development of the four orders of functions and their interaction within the field of the individual person and—as we shall later see— of a culture-whole such as ours.

c. *Functions of the Third Order*

The appearance of the type of activity and consciousness which can be classified as a third order of function may be considered from two different points of view. The usual one in our empirical and materialistic culture directs our attention to what must have outwardly taken place in small tribal societies. On the other hand, from an 'esoteric' point of view, the appearance of the new type of consciousness and activity—thus of a new way of responding and relating to human existence within the biosphere—is interpreted as the result of the impact of a particular type of spiritual energy and will upon an as yet quasi-animal mankind totally subservient to biological drives and unconscious compulsions.

This impact also involved a transcendental and cosmic kind of 'compassion'; we find it mentioned in Greek mythology as Prometheus' gift of divine fire to unself-conscious primitive man. In Hindu mythology, it is pictorialized as the coming to our planet of the Kumaras, a group of spiritual-cosmic Beings from some more advanced realm of existence symbolically referred to as 'Venus'.[2]

---

[2] Venus here need not be thought of as the present planet of that name. The Kumaras may be considered a part of the *spiritual harvest* of evolution in some planetary scheme that long ago (according to the Hindu theosophical tradition, at least 11 million years ago) had reached its "omega point". In this sense, the Kumaras would represent a seed of planetary consciousness and potential energy blown across cosmic space by the winds

The empirical and sociopsychological interpretation of the way in which functions of the third order developed in primitive societies poses but few problems. It is based on expectable reactions of a tribesman to some kind of personal achievement—discovery, invention, or inner revelation—which singled him out and brought him to a position of prestige. This, in turn, led him to the realization (at first temporary, then increasingly accentuated) of being in an uncommon way, *different* from other tribesmen. At first the tribesman in such a position is likely to have considered himself only the mouthpiece or instrument of the tribal god; but admiration, the loving attention of women, and continued success could easily have developed in him a deep feeling of pride in his achievements and inner isolation—the feeling of being 'special' and endowed by his god with a unique status.

On the other hand, if a tribesman felt himself a failure or for some reason could not live up to the expectations of his peers (perhaps because of some special deficiency or deformity), he might also come to regard himself, *in a negative sense,* separate and different from the tribal group. Once emphasized, difference —whether positive or negative—has to be interpreted by the mind. It is given some kind of meaning. It makes a person feel apart from the group, even if only in a subtle way. It produces the sense of being either 'above' or 'outside of' the other members. A sense of detachment, isolation, and in some circumstances, the refusal to submit to common standards because they are felt to no longer apply to one's unique or special case, act as individualizing factors.

A new type of interpersonal relationships takes form when

---

of destiny (karma) and reaching the virgin soil of the Earth—though not the normally *physical* soil, but a far more subtle realm of existence, then as yet undeveloped. The Kumaras *might* have actually come from the subtle realm of the planet Venus after it had "dematerialized", or reached a state of obscuration. If the theory advanced by Velikovsky is at all valid, it could be that a large comet of physical matter would have been drawn into the field of this dematerialized Venus, which as a result would have begun a new cycle of material existence. This hypothesis, wild as it may seem to astronomers, would reconcile the Velikovsky theory and the ancient occult teaching. It may not be more fantastic than some recent astronomical hypotheses.

intertribal contacts and exchanges become more frequent and more complex. As travel, trade, personal acquisition of wealth, and marriage to people of other cultural backgrounds extend the field of consciousness as well as the problems the tribe has ,to face, and above all as large cities are built, an increasing number of human activities lose some of their natural biological character; they become socialized and culturalized in an altogether new way. The city acts as an individualizing frame of reference, even when retaining a relatively homogeneous character. This character gradually loses its strength when slaves become incorporated, even though not integrated, in the city-whole. The relationship of the husband to wife and even of children to parents now living in more clearly defined and often isolated dwellings, changes. City organization calls for specialization.

The image of the autocratic king claiming to represent or even embody what once was the unifying presence of the tribal god also becomes a subconscious and idealized focal point for the growth of the sense of individuality. At first the king's image is glorified by a new kind of religion, non-tribal in character, and his power is supported by a tentacular bureaucracy and police. But the rivalries, corruption and abuses of absolute power result in psychological as well as political upheavals. In time, the people rise and sooner or later, every human being dreams of being a king in his own right. Even though the voice of the divinely inspired Prophet proclaiming that the Kingdom of Heaven is within every human being is stilled and a religious bureaucracy perpetuates itself "in His Name," the new image is not totally forgotten and it eventually makes its mark upon Western society.

The important point in this sketchy historical picture is that the sense of individuality develops in the midst of societies transformed by a new and dynamic kind of mind-activity attempting to deal with new problems of relationship between persons no longer entirely dominated by biological drives or their glorified and universalized symbolic projections. This urge to be and act as an individual, intent on asserting his own at least relatively unique status as an 'I am,' develops both *on the background* of society, religion, and culture, and *against* the inertial power of the type of inbred unanimity of response which, in the old tribal state, was natural and unchallengeable, but in large centralized societies acquires an oppressive character. The result of such a situation is the development of the ego.

If one considers the development of the ego in individuals in terms of its outer perceptible manifestation, this development can be related to the process of imitation (or *mimesis*) characteristic of infancy during the first two years of life. The baby's consciousness is molded by what it feels, perceives, and hears in the family environment. He hears adults referring to him or her as Paul or Jane. He establishes relatively steady patterns of relationship with parents, nurses, or siblings, each of whom asserts his or her character of being as a particular, separate, definable entity. The result is that the very young child begins to claim objects as 'mine' and to say 'I want'. As the child grows up, the 'I-feeling' normally develops in intensity, but in direct relation to the socio-cultural patterns of thinking-feeling-behaving prevalent in the immediate environment. This relation may be positive or negative: the socio-cultural patterns may be accepted passively, adjusted to in search of the maximum pleasure and comfort of the body-as-a-whole, and cleverly used by the developing intelligence which, at this stage, is the servant of biological motivation. Or, the child may respond negatively to environmental pressures, lack of interest or love, or sibling competition and develop an ego polarized by an instinctive reaction *against* the environment.

However, to simply consider the ego as a conscious feeling-realization of being different from other human beings who affect the body-consciousness, but also who can be used and played with for bodily rewards, does not tell the whole story. One must also deal with the manner in which the *manifestation* of the ego appears and develops. These manifestations become more or less set as 'character', but at the root of the feeling of 'I' we should postulate what I have called 'the self'. This word, self, has a very ambiguous character and has been given a great variety of meanings. As I use the term, the self is the power that establishes the particular nature, the essential character and the vibratory frequency of a living organism.

In the animal kingdom the self is generic, not individualized.

All the members of a species have but one self, common to all. Selfhood is not differentiated or particularized. There are superficial differences between the members of the species, but fundamentally, the species-as-a-whole alone has a self. All its members are rooted in it. It is a generic power.

In human beings, however, selfhood is *potentially* individualized. There is a generic self referring to the characteristics of *homo sapiens;* but at the core of every human being, an individual self is present as a latent power. Self is power, not consciousness. Consciousness is the expression of the wholeness of the organic field of activity we call a human being; but at first, consciousness is purely biological, because 'life' is the basic sustaining power. Something has to be added to life to bring out the possibility of individualized selfhood. According to all traditions, this 'something'—to which I have often referred as the 'God-seed'— results from the action of superior, Earth-transcending entities. It is the previously mentioned Promethean gift.

The ego has been defined by Carl Jung as the center of the field of consciousness, and also as its circumference. If the ego is considered as a power of integration, it is so only as *the reflection* of the self. The ego is not power, but only the reflection of power at the center of the field of consciousness. The ego is actually far more occupied with what occurs at the circumference than at the center, for it is at the circumference of his or her being that a person faces, and in some manner has to react or respond to the pressure and impacts of the social, cultural, and biospheric environment. The ego is, in fact, *a mechanism* of adjustment to the socio-cultural environment. Yet this mechanism implies the existence of a sustaining power—the self—which gives to the mechanism its essential purpose and in some way can make its presence felt, even if the ego does not realize what this power is. Without the operative, even though subconscious and 'occult' presence of this self, the ego could not challenge the compulsion of 'life' operating as biological instincts. But the ego is not aware of the source of the power enabling it to resist instinctual drives which no animal can disobey.

The ego is involved in, and concerned only with, mechanisms and techniques of adjustments to, or control of, the environment. By the use of intellectual faculties—which at first manifest as cunning—it discovers its capacity to affect other people and material things so as to increase its pleasures or comfort and to avoid pain. The ego thus acts as a technician, an engineer. But while it uses the mind as an instrument, it also finds itself molded by, and often the prisoner of, the mind. The mind's activities bind the ego—somewhat like a political ruler or executive often finds himself thwarted by the bureaucracy through which he has to operate. The ego not only becomes subservient to the mechanisms it is using (the mind), but most of the time its motives and goals are dictated—whether it realizes it or not —by biological drives and by the social and ethical imperatives of the culture in which it has developed, or by an emotional and often blind rebellion against either biology or culture.

Yet, behind this rebellion, or even behind the ego's ambition to fulfill a particular aspect of the culture in an original and fame-producing manner, stands the power of the self. The self in man is the individualizer. Because of its presence, the ego can develop within the mind-field, giving to that field centrality and a particular structure. Still, the ego (at least for a long time) is not aware of the self as the source of its power; it is too occupied with what it is doing and with handling situations which constantly pose problems of adjustment or offer new opportunities for expansion and mastery over the environment.

In contrast to this restless and multifarious activity of the ego, the self simply is—what it is. It is the power required to fulfill the purpose (or *dharma*) inherent in the fact that a *human* being is born at a certain place and a particular time. Because it is 'human', this being is not only endowed with life, but with the potentiality of consciously fulfilling a particular role within the planetary field of the Earth *as an individual self*. In order to actualize this potentiality, the diffuse consciousness characterizing the prehuman levels of evolution has to become structured and centralized. The process of structuring takes place through the development of culture (second order of function), but culture centralizes the consciousness of a *collectivity* of human beings (a community). At this stage, centralization is, in a sense, outside of any particular person. As the power of the self asserts itself more strongly within a few individuals, and at the same time outer circumstances pressure these individuals into developing a sense of superiority or of relative isolation (and perhaps alienation) from their community, the consciousness of these individuals begins to centralize itself. The more 'special' the activities of these persons and their responses to social pressures, the more insistently the feeling of internal centrality is experienced. But this feeling remains conditioned by outer circumstances and activities; it is attached to them, and the result is the development of an ego so concerned with what occurs at the circumference of the field that it cannot be aware of what is at the root of this 'I-feeling'.

Considered from the point of view of the evolution of mankind, two factors combine to produce the ego. On the one hand, the ego is the product of changing conditions and increasing complexities in the development of culture-wholes. There is also the activation of the potentiality of individual selfhood—a potentiality which, I repeat, tradition claims to have been imparted long ago to primitive, animal-like mankind by Promethean beings. Yet, as far as our present humanity is concerned, it is only since about 600 B. C. that the development of an objective intellectual-analytical mind, at least theoretically detached from biology and culture, began to affect the collective life of human societies. The activity of this mind manifests in numerous ways, and I refer to them as functions of the third order.

Our Western society, especially since the European Renaissance, has been the first to conspicuously feature ideals and concepts of organization based on such a type of functional activity. The result has been the extraordinarily rapid growth of modern science and technology, and the spread of democratic institutions, at least, theoretically proclaiming the worth and dignity of the individual person and legalizing individual rights, in principle without any biological (sex, color, race) or cultural (class, caste, wealth-state) qualifications. Our Western society has glorified 'rugged individualism' and an uncontrolled freedom of operation and personal ambition under the name of *laissez-faire*. It has become a society *of* egos, *by* egos and *for* the greater glory of egos under the pretense of allowing full uninhibited self-expression and 'self-actualization'. It is a society which has also become hypnotized by technology and mechanisms of all types. The ego depends upon mechanisms and techniques in order to be active at the circumference of existence; and it finds excitement and justification for its passion for controlling everything and everyone in an activity aggressively directed *against* whatever is an obstacle to its 'freedom' or whatever challenges the validity of the set patterns of thinking-feeling defined by the mind over which it rules. Yet, this multifarious ego-activity fills a necessary function in the development of mankind. Through ego-activity, the process of evolution continues to transform human consciousness, freeing it from total subservience to biological compulsions and from attachment to the rigid traditions and limiting world-view of a particular culture.

What the ego believes to be 'freedom' is, nevertheless, anarchy. It expresses the negative and catabolic aspect of civilization; and it flourishes in a paradoxical way in our modern megalopoles—paradoxical in that ego-freedom soon turns into a tragic state of bondage to the compulsion to feel free, independent and self-motivated at any cost. The true kind of autonomy is only found in the self. The self does not need to 'prove' itself free and autonomous. It is what it is, without any concern about what this particular 'is-ness' implies in relation to other kinds of 'is-ness'. There is no concern because true selfhood does not refer to consciousness or relationship, but only to power—the power to be what one is. Yet, this power does not operate in isolation. It represents one small but precise vibration (or tone) in the immense chord of mankind. But this small tone vibrates at a level that transcends the mind and its techniques and categories.

The ego does not function at that level; it only reflects what takes place there. But in doing that reflecting it brings the supernatural reality to a state of consciousness which can be formulated and transferred. The ego, and all third-order functions which refer to the conscious mind, work in two ways. All these activities, consciously or not, strive to raise human consciousness from the biological-cultural level to the 'spiritual' level. In their noblest forms these activities *infuse* spirit into biology and culture. But this means breaking down the particularity and exclusivity inherent in any culture-whole—as culture-wholes have been so far—and opening the collective (as well as the individual) mind to a state of total *in*clusiveness and interpenetration.

This breaking-down process can take many forms. Some are catharses leading to a radical repolarization of the mind and a transmutation of biological energies and socio-cultural allegiances; others have seemingly, or at least temporarily, destructive results. It is because this process is potentially so dangerous in the atmosphere of our city-civilization that it can best be experienced on the individual level within the extended field of vibration (or aura) of human beings who, having passed at least to some degree through the process, radiate a holistic and compassionate spirituality that accepts every human function as partial means to the realization of a state of multi-level, polyphonic development. In such 'trans-individual' personages, functions of the *fourth order* operate. In due time these functions will bring about a new condition of transhuman existence in which biology will be transcended or transfigured. Men will gradually lose their personal ambition, their pride of achievement and their catabolic jealousies, and culture will lose its collective focusing on exclusivity.

In that state of existence, love—having overcome biological compulsiveness, its culture-bred class distinctions and egocentric insecurity and possessiveness—will be able to flourish in unpolluted radiance and pan-harmonic inclusiveness. It will be the foundation upon which function of the fourth order will develop and a new world will be built. The earth will become a *garden* reflecting the many-sided inner culture of integrated human persons no longer needing wilderness to balance and redeem the artificiality of their ego-minds. The spiritual darkness of our festering megalopoles will be forgotten then. Then human beings, in a much reduced number, will celebrate their common divinity in 'Holy Cities.'

d. *Functions of the Fourth Order*

This seemingly utopian picture most likely should not be taken as describing an even relatively imminent situation. If occult traditions are valid indicators of time periods—and there is always the possibility that they are of a more symbolic than actual or 'historical' character—the Promethean gift of the 'fire of individual selfhood' and reflective consciousness to mankind occurred millions of years ago. The *seed-potentiality* of developing an individualizing mind and a centralizing ego-function was released into the Earth's biosphere when the culture-developing functions of the second order were beginning to operate on a definite scale. Therefore, this 'seed' took a very long time to 'germinate'. It may also be that there was a first (and unsuccessful) germination under very adverse karmic 'weather', and that —in the fabled Atlantis—the first germ was frozen. A second attempt had to be made after some symbolic or actual 'Deluge'.

The functions of the third order have now reached a peak in their development; but once more mankind is experiencing a dangerous state of planet-wide, all-human infection produced by the inordinate glorification of—and dependence upon—intellectual fragmentation and ego-ambition. We have no way of knowing where it will lead, but we may well say that this potentially tragic condition was predictable. In a sense, it was inherent in the radically revolutionary approach to existence promoted by Guatama the Buddha, and by a few Greek philosopher-seers, especially Pythagoras. On the other hand, the Buddha (and probably Pythagoras) not only focused and released the transforming seminal power of an objective, rational and independently self-controlled mental activity, the very nature of this Buddha-focus also implied, and should have revealed, a mind-and-culture-transcending *love* for mankind—indeed, a Promethean kind of compassion.

This *implied* compassion had to be made explicit. The energy of an all-inclusive 'divine' love became focused in India, at least at a mental level, in the ideal of the *Boddhisattva* who renounces the spiritual freedom and supermental state of Nirvana until *all sentient creatures* (i.e., all living organisms in the Earth's biosphere) have reached such a condition of being and consciousness. A century after the Boddhisattva ideal began to spread through Northern India, this energy of supreme love became definitely embodied in the person of Jesus and was released to the world under the mystic name of Christ, through the potent symbol of the Crucifixion. This *Christ* gift can thus be compared to the Promethean gift; the latter referring to the release of the seed-potentiality of objective, metabiological mind-activity and of consciousness centered in individual self-hood, the former to the release of the seed-potentiality of an all-inclusive, universal, and divine love of which the Christian *agape* is a reflection.

Such a love is only *the feeling aspect* of the foundation upon which functions of the fourth order must develop, if their activity operates in a positive manner—i.e., along the direction of the evolutionary process leading to the state of seed-consummation, the omega state.[3] The foundation for the development of functions of the fourth order has also a *mental* aspect—mind as a field of holistic (rather than atomistic) activity, mind as a formative power operating according to the principle of inclusion, and no longer of exclusion.

The analytical mind creates categories in which many events, biological characteristics, or experimental data are classified according to their common *external features;* it is so intent on making its data fit into the categories that it automatically ex-

---

[3] Any function at any level of activity can operate in a negative way; thus, in opposition to the direction the evolutionary process takes at any point of a cycle. A cell or organ can become cancerous, developing uncontrolled against the holistic power of the organism-as-a-whole. A society and its culture can split and become fragmented into rival groups. An individual person can break down in psychosis as it becomes the battlefield on which individualizing trends war against socio-cultural inertia or the insistent demands of repressed biopsychic functions. So also the Christian *agape*, haunted by an emotionalized ideal of 'salvation', can degenerate into the fanaticism manifesting as the Medieval Inquisition, torturing bodies to save souls. More details concerning the dualism of evolutionary and anti-evolutionary forces will be found in *The Planetarization of Consciousness*, Part 2.

cludes—or at least considers totally unimportant and meaning-less—whatever does not easily fit. On the other hand, the holistic (or spiritually synthesizing) mind works with *basic principles of organization* formulated in such a broad manner that they can include a vast number of data or activities which, while they may appear externally unrelated, nevertheless stem from a single *root-reality* or original creative impulse. Such an aspect of the human mind develops through the operation of what, many years ago, I called *the cosmogenic function.*

'Cosmos' means order, harmony and beauty. The cosmogenic mind is able not only to discover cosmos with and through chaos; it sees beauty in seeming ugliness. It can also act as a catalyst of order. Such a mind operates beyond the conflict between what lesser minds hypnotized by ethical-cultural differences consider 'good' and 'evil'; it sees both polarities as necessary for the continued release of power—just as no drawing can exist without a contrast between dark lines and light background.

Behind *agape*-love and the holistic, cosmogenic mind stands the principle of *interpenetration.* At the level of a fourth order type of functional activity, all forms of existence begin to interpenetrate. At that level, ego-exclusivity, emotional possessiveness, and intellectual pride lose their power and glamor. They are seen to be only temporary means in the long and arduous process of differentiating human personalities, of stabilizing the relationship of center to circumference (and vice versa) and thus developing in depth an inner feeling of I-am-ness. They seem to be inevitable by-products of the emergence and full-growth of objective and reflective self-consciousness out of the matrices of biology and culture; but once their work is nearly finished, all these mental ego-building and ego-generated forms of mental activity should lose their opaqueness and mass. They should overcome their subservience to the concept of 'physicality' that served to integrate and stabilize sense-experiences and bio-psychic feelings. Mind and ego should become *translucent,* allowing the light of the future and last state of human evolution—its omega condition—to pour through them. This pouring through of the omega radiance—which, for the Christian mystic, is identified with the cosmic Christ—must, in time, *transfigure* the biological into the spiritual. Enlightenment in its highest form means literally becoming light, which the radiance of saints and mystics prefigures.

Since the beginning of the 20th century, various movements have attempted to formulate—in terms of the present *need* of a humanity hypnotized by the intellectual and technological achievements of our Western civilization—concepts and ideals of emotional and mental transformation. In India, the great philosopher, poet, seer and yogi—Sri Aurobindo—saw himself faced with a twofold task. He questioned the significance and value of the several ways in which Hindu spirituality had developed for a very long time, and he sought to clarify and re-energize India's inner life, deeply shaken by the intrusion of Western thinking, by a vivid reinterpretation of the most ancient sources of Hinduism—the Vedas and the Upanishads. He went further and attempted to do what the Rishis of Vedic times could not do because of the purely biological level at which human tribes then operated, but had now become possible: that is, a direct, publicly formulated and personally dramatized focusing of the energy of the *"Supermind"*—the highest level of consciousness and spiritual realization open to mankind. What had presumably been available only to a few exceptional personages was, he felt, now a possible answer to a general, planet-wide human need, varied as the outer forms of the need might be. He sought to implant the germinal realization of the Supermind—which he and his partner in the Great Work, Mother Mira, had experienced—*into the soil of the entire biosphere,* even at the level of a transphysical manifestation.

In the Euro-American world, the formulation of concepts and ideals of emotional and mental transformation has begun to take place within the framework of science. On the one hand, modern atomic and subatomic physics since Einstein has been revealing a totally new and, so far, bewildering world far more 'transphysical' than physical.

In the field of psychology, after the spread of the catabolic and reductionist (even if emotionally releasing) Freudian psychoanalysis, came the 'Humanistic' movement. Humanistic psychologists have attempted to show that it is possible (and not even extraordinarily so) for human beings to experience states of consciousness beyond the limiting patterns built-up by the socio-cultural and intellectual functions of the third order and the ego. C. G. Jung began this process when he outlined a "healing way" out of neurosis and spiritual frustration by allowing the consciousness to open up to a vast realm of symbols and archetypes. Then Abraham Maslow, by concentrating on the study of the "peak experiences" of healthy and self-actualizing individuals, helped to reassess and redefine in psychological terms the components of a wholesome and harmonic kind of individualism. Recently, a further step toward developing the functions of the fourth order has been taken through 'Transpersonal psychology'. With Transpersonal psychology the attempt has been to carefully and as objectively as possible investigate, and then formulate the main characteristics of, ego-and-intellect-transcending states of consciousness which have been traditionally catalogued as 'mystical'.

It seems that the time has now come to present in as concrete and understandable a form as possible a new 'model' (the now current scientific term) of reality. This reality is gradually becoming more perceptible to the collective mind of a large number of thinking individuals because of the immensely expanded scope and transcendent implications of human activity. And I am not referring here only to a physical type of body-activity, but as well to consciously directed changes and processes operating at the level of the holistic mind—the mind of wholeness, the mind able not only to perceive events occurring in the sky, but to develop a 'cosmic' sense in relation to *every* human experience. I speak of a cosmic mind because it spontaneously and intuitively interprets any experience according to a holistic frame of reference according to which there is no *essential* difference between microcosm and macrocosm.

Whether man sees and defines them as small or vast, all organized fields of interdependent activities are existential wholes structured by principles which can best be called 'cosmic'. Though this often carelessly used and abused term may confuse some people, there seems to be no more appropriate qualificative to characterize mental processes (and some ritualized physical acts) which today must be clearly differentiated from the activities of biologically and culturally conditioned individuals (or groups), operating basically according to personal-emotional, ego-determined, and ethico-rational imperatives.

At the stage of mental development reached by mankind today, a profound, planet-wide need for *the cosmification* of human understanding and collective processes is making itself felt in a myriad of ways. Human life and human society should be repolarized and radically transformed by a cosmic meaning. But this meaning is not a 'given' one. It is not 'natural' in a biological, socio-cultural or strictly personal (ego-conditioned) sense. It has to be *implanted* or grafted to the ordinary consciousness of every human being by visionary individuals whose minds are becoming increasingly able to focus and release into a humanity in crisis the power and consciousness of what as yet is man's future state of evolution.

Mystics and metaphysicians may wish to speak of that future as 'here and now' in a timeless condition of 'being'; but such statements are the results either of ineffable but *transitory* experiences in moments of ecstasy, or of strictly intellectual and formalistic speculation largely dealing with negative concepts in an attempt to formulate the rationally unformulatable. Yet, the basic and incontrovertible fact of existence is change—which, as man experiences it, implies rhythmic motion and the incessant (or at least periodic) alteration of organized fields of activity and forms of consciousness. We cannot deny existence, because to deny it implies the existence of the denier—which negates the original denial of existence. A complete denial of existence is never possible because *something* (or somebody) existing has to make such a denial. We can only change the character and scope, the quality and intensity of our perceptions (inner or outer) and our interpretations.

For many centuries, man's perceptions have been defined and interpreted by what we might call a *physicogenic function*. The operation of that function synthesizes the many data provided by our senses and some inner organismic feelings. As a result, our physical world is produced—a world of material bodies (whether atoms, cells, human beings or celestial bodies), a world of separate 'particles' attracting or repelling each other. A newly developing human function is now seeking to *re*define and *re*interpret man's immensely extended environment in a new transphysical, transpersonal, super-rationalistic and symbolic manner. This *'cosmogenic function'* constitutes the central aspect of the holistic mind.

As already stated, this function characterizes the activity of a mind operating in multidimensional fields of existence according to the principle of total inclusiveness. As a result of this kind of operation, man's consciousness perceives everywhere 'cosmoi'—interdependent and interpenetrating existential wholes. What constitutes a cosmos is not its size in space and time— whether it is an atom or a galaxy—but rather its essential character of total inclusiveness, even if a human consciousness seeking to embrace the actual totality of its manifestation falls very short of encompassing its entire field of activity. In that field and at any level of existence, all pairs of opposites, even that of actuality and potentiality (or being and non-being) should always be included.

What the modern Western mind defines as 'cosmology' is not, in the above-defined sense, truly 'cosmic', because it takes for granted that the universe it describes is exclusively physical. It therefore excludes the possibility of non-physical (whether sub- or super-physical) forms of existence as components of what it calls 'reality'. Moreover, implicitly if not explicitly, it still assumes that man, the observer, is in some undefined manner *exterior* to the astronomical processes he observes. Even if the modern cosmologist is religiously inclined, in most cases he also assumes, according to the tradition of his culture, that God created the universe by an act of will and imagination, and remains essentially *outside* of His creation. Such a fundamental 'outsideness' has no place in a truly cosmic vision of reality, according to the meaning I give here to this term, 'cosmic'. For a human consciousness fully operating at the level of functions of the fourth order, there can be no absolute outside—simply because every existential whole interpenetrates within the finite field of cosmic activity.

As every whole is part of a greater whole and contains parts which, as wholes, have parts, etc., there can ultimately be nothing outside. Each existential whole has its own space-field and time-span (cycle) insofar as it acts as a whole; but it also is subjected to the rhythms of the larger whole in which it operates as a part. That operation is *structurally defined* by these larger rhythms. Thus, while every living organism (human being included) has a biological rhythm of its own, determined by its total genetic ancestry, the overall development of its biological and psychic functions is also conditioned and constantly influenced by the pulsating and periodical rhythms of the planet Earth in the activity of which it participates—and also of the whole solar system (or *heliocosm*) whose power-center is the sun.

The phrase 'functions of the fourth order' refers to all the activities which, within the total field constituting *a whole person*—and not merely what we now interpret as a physical body limited to the skin or an ego-structured psyche—relate, on a consciously all-inclusive basis, the individual to the whole of which he (or she) accepts to act as a part.[4] The conscious development of such a relationship, and the discovery of all it implies, is what the 'cosmogenic function' is all about. In terms of its larger and potentially all-inclusive unfoldment, this function should produce, no longer a physicality-obsessed cosmology, but an all-inclusive multi-dimensional *cosmosophy*.

The mystic usually reaches the transcendent realization of a 'unitive state' of consciousness, beyond duality and the ordinary space-time framework of present-day human existence, by an intense *chiaroscuro of feelings* in which intensely dark, torturing periods precede (and at times also follow) moments of ecstatic illumination and bliss. He or she experiences to the utmost the great dramas of transcendent and absolute love, and lives in their most extreme forms the alternating emotions to which total union and seemingly irrevocable separation (or deep-seated guilt) give rise. In the unitive state, the mystic feels that all

---

[4] My book, *The Planetarization of Consciousness,* in which my whole philosophy of existence is contained in seed, has the subtitle *From the Individual to the Whole;* but few readers seem to have paid attention to this subtitle.

is included, all is one; yet the fundamental experience at the root of all experience—change—is denied. In timelessness all processes are invalidated, illusory. Only the greatest mystics reach beyond repudiating existence and realize that *nirvana* and *samsara* are but two aspects of an ineffable reality in which potentiality and actuality interact.

A 'cosmosophist' seeks to understand these interactions so as to move along the tide of evolution. He (or she) deals with *the movement*, instead of negating it in subjective experiences of timelessness and ecstasy. He deals with cyclicity rather than the separate phases of cycles. He deals with principles, rather than empirical phenomena which, he realizes, can only reveal their essential meaning and value when apprehended and understood in terms of *their place and function* within a whole process. Thus, for the cosmosophist, an individual seen under a 'cosmic' light appears as *the representative* of a particular phase of the cyclic process of human evolution. The individual's task (*dharma* or truth-of-being) is to bring to a focus in himself and through his activity what that particular phase is meant to accomplish in terms of the purpose of the entire process. *As a person*, he is a whole; but the wholeness of that whole takes its essential meaning from *the position* the person occupies within a larger whole in which he acts as a functional part.

What then is the larger whole of which an individual human being can consciously and significantly realize himself a functional part?

For countless millennia, no human being living in primitive tribal conditions could think of, much less feel and actually experience his participation in a 'greater whole' larger than his tribe. Later on, the field of an effective and realistic possibility of experienced participation extended to a province, then a kingdom, then a nation. Today, circumglobal travel, the astronauts' experiences of seeing Earth as a distant globe—shared by millions of TV viewers—and the publicizing of the interdependence of all forms of life within the biosphere have made it possible for people to be aware of the lives and sufferings of all human beings. Any well-informed, sensitive individual can now consider both humanity and the Earth as the greater whole in reference to which he (or she) can motivate and give meaning and value to his thinking, feeling and behavior. If he does so, the functions of the fourth order begin to operate. They operate now within the field of a consciousness that, having previously been individualized, is able to formulate itself with an objectivity and precision that were not possible *before* the functions of the third order had at least partially and effectively developed.

At the biological level, the sense of participation in a larger whole is unconscious and compulsive. At the socio-cultural level, it is collectivistic and subconsciously and emotionally binding; what is more, it is rooted in the principle of exclusion of the alien. At the level of the process of individualization, this sense of participation tends to disappear from the field of consciousness. Its reappearance, even in an attenuated and partial form, indicates that functions of the fourth order are becoming operative. All-inclusive, compassionate love and the activity of the cosmogenic mind are the two pillars upon which the entire development of these functions rests.

For a long time in the evolution of individual and even more of collective forms of consciousness, these pillars lack firmness and total reliability as supports of human activity. To love *all* human beings is very difficult in many situations. The Boddhisattva ideal of not only loving all human beings, but accepting an immensely long series of incarnations out of compassion for all living organisms, must seem even more unrealistic to all but an exceedingly few human beings, if they *really* understood and vividly experienced through feelings what this implies. Such an ideal must rest upon the total realization that the Earth is not only a living organism, but that humanity as a whole has a functional role to perform in it. Mankind performs that 'planetary' function through the operation of a long series of different kinds of societies and culture. Every 'culture-whole' represents a particular aspect of this function.

As I see it, this 'human function'—which we might call the archetype, Man—consists of formulating, in mental and in concrete cultural terms, the meaning and value of *every kind* of activity operating within the entire planetary field of activity— a field which probably extends as far as the moon's orbit (what long ago was called the 'sublunar' realm—in a sense, the Earth's aura). Thus, mankind's function could be considered analogous to that of the several nervous systems in a human body. It implies far more than an accurate observation and meaningful interpretation of existential phenomena. Inherent in it is the possibility of not merely affecting, but, for better or for worse, radically transforming the operation of the various factors active within the entire planetary field.

We should now be well aware that mankind can pollute and might even destroy that field. Man can do it because, for so many centuries, he has been made to believe that essentially he did not belong to the Earth, a planet of conflicts and sorrows. He had been told (Genesis I:28) that the whole world was made for him to deal with as he pleased—or that it was a school in which he had to learn arduous lessons. As long as the human mind holds this kind of thought or feeling-inducing imagery, and clings to it as a principle on which to base its conduct, it will be impossible for functions of the fourth order even to operate, let alone operate effectively.

Nevertheless, at one time this Biblical principle—which undoubtedly has equivalents in other cultures, but certainly not in all of them—had evident validity. It was needed to assist the process of individualization (functions of the third order). Human beings had to feel themselves essentially separate from nature in order that the whole energy of their collective (as well as individual) growth could be focused upon the development of the analytical, objective and rationalistic mind.

Today, however, mankind is faced by the dire results of such a collective attitude to which a religious sanction gave so much strength. The developing world-crisis can be successfully met —and first of all, understood—if at least the 'creative minority' (Arnold Toynbee's term) of mankind is able to overcome and transcend this basic concept of alienation and separateness from the Earth-as-a-whole; yet at the same time, man should retain the capacity to clearly formulate through some kind of evocative and potentially transformative language—i.e., through some new type of organization of symbols—the meaning he now sees emerging from nuclear physics, galactic astronomy and international and intergroup relationships. The new language will evolve from the operation of the functions of the fourth order, and particularly from the cosmogenic function. But that function must no longer work in some kind of a human vacuum, as its first manifestations along purely abstract, scientific lines have done. It has to be open to the illumination which an all-pervasive Christic or Boddhisattvic love-compassion can bestow, or at the intellectual level, to what the potentially transforming concept of *interpenetration* can provide, if wholly and irrevocably accepted by man's total being.

3

FUNCTIONS OF TRANSITION AND RITES OF PASSAGE

In attempting to outline the character of functions of the four orders or levels of human activity, I purposely made only passing reference to the kind of functions which, though still belonging to a lower order of which they are the culmination, serve as a matrix or seed out of which the 'higher' functions emerge, gradually unfolding their until-then latent potentialities. In the past, Western science sharply distinguished between inanimate and animate entities, and established definite levels of organic complexity and activity called the mineral, vegetable, animal and human kingdoms. Today we realize that the evolutionary process of which we can be aware is a continuum, and we perceive systems of organization which to some extent partake of the characteristics of life in two kingdoms or can be interpreted as transitory developments between them. In many instances, no very clear distinction can be made between inorganic and organic, or between vegetable and animal; and we increasingly realize that attributes and forms of activity in individuals and collectivities we so long thought to be exclusively human are at least clearly prefigured in a number of animal species.

What often seems to most strikingly characterize our species is the capacity inherent in a human being to pass *consciously* through radical and often critical processes of transformation and to reach higher levels of existence; nevertheless there are numerous instances of animal metamorphoses, the most noted and mythologized one being that of the worm into chrysalis and butterfly. However, these animal metamorphoses apparently differ in nature from the transformation processes through which human beings can pass. Human metamorphoses—at least as we can experience and perceive them with our present-day consciousness—operate more specifically in terms of consciousness and of the character and quality of interpersonal and socio-cultural relationships; still, definite physiological changes are involved in mental-spiritual transformation, and it may be unwise to believe that mankind may not exist in a *transphysical* state, at a still very remote period of its future evolution.

We do not know what brings about animal metamorphoses or what purpose they serve in the overall balance of the biosphere; but we can, to some extent, follow in individual human beings, the evolution of mankind as a whole, and in the development of a particular society or culture-whole, the manner in which the process of transformation takes place at this time. We can see it operate from step to step, as it passes from one level of activity and of consciousness to the next; we can be aware of the use of functions of transition as effective means for transformation.

I shall now attempt to analyze and define the nature of the functions of transition which appear to be essential links in the development of human beings from the first to the second, the second to the third, and the third to the fourth orders of functional activities. Later, we shall see how what can be experienced by individuals is also implied in the evolution of mankind as a whole; and how, because humanity is evidently at a critical point of its evolution today, the possibility of a transformation of the consciousness of a large number of individuals, whose lives have become uprooted and de-structured by far-reaching social-mental changes, is a most significant factor with which to reckon.

a. *Sex as a Seed Function*

The fundamental difference between the sexual function and other biological functions—like breathing, digesting, blood-circulation and infection fighting by directing white blood-cells wherever needed—is that sexual activity (at least in its natural state) requires the interaction of two organisms, polarized for the purpose of biological reproduction. The above-mentioned functions are *intraorganic;* sex is an *interorganic* process. It sets into operation the principles of external relatedness. The various organs of a body are related to each other; so, too, are their specific activities. They often act as pairs of opposites, particularly in the case of the sympathetic and parasympathetic nervous systems, and some endocrine glands—for instance, the insulin-producing part of the pancreas and the adrenals. But this pairing (or complementary action) operates within one single organism, while the essential characteristic of sexual activity is to bring together two organisms, and biologically speaking, two sets of genes and two ancestral lines—thus producing a more complex situation.

Sex therefore represents the potentiality of an ever-increasing biological *complexity*. Its evolutionary purpose is to produce ever more complex variations on the theme of 'Man'—the archetype of human nature as we know it today, *Homo sapiens*. This process of compounding complexity requires the interaction not merely of a male and female. It requires organisms which have become, on the one hand, differentiated in their organismic responses to the environment, but on the other hand, not so greatly different from each other in their respective biological (and later on in human evolution, socio-cultural) patterns of responses; otherwise they would introduce a particular line of evolutionary development variations too centrifugal and unassimilable. The need for differentiation accounts for the apparently universal rule against incest; that for not *too great* disparity is reflected in the often violent opposition to marriage between a man and a woman of different color, race, tribe or even culture.

The balance between 'enough' and 'not too much' difference in interpersonal relationship is the most important factor to consider in the discussion of marriage as a socio-cultural institution; but it is equally basic a factor to take into account when we think of sex as a function of transition between the first order and the second order of functions—between biology and culture. At the strictly biological level, sex can be reduced to indiscriminate mating between male and female organisms. These organisms act merely as *carriers of seed*—sperm and ovum. The process of biological differentiation is uncontrolled, except by the difficulty for a female organism to be impregnated by a male belonging to a very different species. Yet this difficulty may not have been as great during the early stages of human evolution as it is now, presumably because, as a disciple of Teilhard de Chardin might say, the development of the 'noosphere' (functions of second and third order) has affected the wild and at first totally exuberant rhythms of the primordial 'biosphere'. Even in the tropical regions of the present-day biosphere, this exuberance of the reproductive and expansive power of 'life' in its raw, uncultured state is almost certainly but a pale and greatly attenuated reflection of what it must have been in the days of great reptiles and giant vegetation.

According to occult traditions, human beings too were of gigantic size, and their intense sexual potency could be used for magical purposes of a magnitude of which we can barely dream. This means that the energies aroused by the new factor of interorganismic relationship arising from the polarization of the central power of 'life'—and the power of *self-multiplication*—nearly exploded within an 'adolescent' Earth. That power may have been originally as powerful as the 'binding force' holding together atomic structures; and indeed the self-multiplying organismic power of *life,* and the binding force at work in the kind of system of activity we call *matter* may have to be considered as polar opposites, even though some biological processes have also an integrative character.

In the early phases of planetary evolution, what we now refer to as intense volcanic activity represented an unstabilized and explosive state of atomic-molecular activity. Once it was stabilized, the forms which this energy had acquired then developed inertia, constituting what we now call the mineral kingdom. Then the power inherent in the planet Earth—considered as a vast field of cosmic activity—became focused into biological processes displaying an equally intense explosiveness, but at a new level of organization. At first that explosiveness presumably operated through the process of 'mitosis'—one cell dividing into two, each of which divided into two, etc. This is self-multiplication in simple geometric progression. Much later, when sexual differentiation began, this same primordial energy of life became focused into the process of sexual relatedness.

Thus, sexual reproduction characterizes the culminating phase in the development of strictly biological functions. It seems that, at every level, activity has at first a unitary character; at the level of life, this is self-multiplication through mitosis. Then activity assumes a *bipolar* aspect. The factor of relationship enters the stage of existence. It may be an unimpressive entrance; but as the two polarities gradually assert their difference of rhythm more powerfully, which in turn produces more definitely distinct and complementary forms (organs), a *passion of relatedness* develops.[1] The intensity of that 'passion' and of the power it released in archaic times on continents probably long since disappeared can hardly be realized by our modern, self-conscious mentality today. That power became the foundation of what is today unspectacularly evoked in somewhat anachronistic ceremonies as 'sex magic'.

Once the principle of relatedness begins to manifest in the relationship between two opposite and complementary polarities, a further development is inevitable. Duality leads to plurality or multiplicity; the many-sided relationships of the socio-cultural state absorb some of the wild and at first uncontrollable intensity of bipolar sexual relationships. The 'group' spreads out, controls, and puts to use the energy generated by the polarized 'pairs' it relates in ever larger patterns of organization. As the level of socio-cultural activity is reached, functions of the second order develop. These grow out of the raw material of sexual relatedness.

For its full development, such a growth requires that the evolution of life has reached the animal and, more specifically, the human stage. Sexuality operates in the vegetable kingdom, but primarily in a passive manner, because plants have very little capacity for movement; and the factor of relatedness can

---

[1] It may well be that electrical energy, with its 'positive' and 'negative' polarization, is the secondary manifestation of a still more primary power which had a unitary character. A similar sequence may also characterize the development of mind as a form of consciousness.

operate most significantly only where there is motion—whether it be at the physical or the mental level of activity. Many vegetable species require external assistance for pollenation—wind, birds, or insects. The factor of relatedness begins to have a dynamic character in the animal kingdom; and, having the capacity for 'motion', animals can also experience emotions.

In the human kingdom, the dynamic character of interorganismic relationship acquires a new dimension; sex ceases to be a strictly seasonal activity for an exclusively generic purpose. Sexual interactions may occur at any time; at the mental level, they may span several generations. They may acquire an entirely personal and voluntary character; or they may be impersonal, idealistic and body-transcending. While sex remains the foundation of human relationship, its energy nevertheless becomes increasingly subservient to socio-cultural processes and the promptings of metabiological concepts and values. Motherhood, nursing, the care of the progeny spread over many years, and the building of a home and educational facilities extend, diversify and make more permanent the patterns of relationship which began with mating. In these sex-inspired activities which form the basis of social order, the female is at first the positive and directing factor; she normally rules over the realm of essential duality and polarity. On the other hand, the male deals primarily with the realm of plurality in relationship—the realm of social and group organization. He also develops a technology of sex, and of sex-transformation or sublimation!

As the *psychic overtones* of sex are being developed—whether deliberately by self-control, or unwillingly through natural and social frustration—biological energies are transmuted into socio-cultural drives. These belong to the second order of functions. Man's attention shifts from the fundamental of sex relationship to a great variety of socio-cultural overtones. This shift is an essential feature in the development of a significant and productive culture, and for the preservation of the social order. It manifests as the glorification of chastity and, in some special cases, asceticism. However, it can have detrimental and psychologically or socially destructive results if it is based on a completely negative attitude toward sex, or on a sense of functional inferiority or impotency. Modern depth psychology has stressed, and often over-emphasized, this very real possibility and its multiple consequences. At any rate, the relationship between biological functions (first order) and socio-cultural functions (second order) largely depends upon the attitude which a society has toward sex.

Sex indeed represents a 'critical state' in human evolution; and the period when the development of the sexual function begins, normally at puberty, has been considered in all cultures as a turning point of major importance. In primitive societies where the sex instinct was given relatively full play—except for some specific taboos—the crisis of puberty occupied a very special place and was given a 'sacred' character through puberty rites. These marked the transition between childhood and at least potential adulthood.

Much has been written concerning puberty rites in primitive tribal societies, and the part played by divine Beings impersonated by shamans, medicine-men, or simply men of a certain clan has been described. But ethnologists have recorded primarily the external features of these rites; and these men, trained in the 'scientific' techniques of detached and objective observation, have often lacked the ability to meaningfully relate the dramatic, violent, and often bloody ceremonies to the entire process of human unfoldment from one level of activity to the next. They have seen that what was dramatized in the puberty rituals was a process of death to the old and rebirth to a new phase of existence and consciousness, but the important point in the process is the respective character of, and the basic relationship between, the two phases; thus the meaning of the transition from the *natural* state of childhood to that of participation in a *socio-cultural whole*—from 'life' to 'culture'. What is most important for us to understand is the fact that all cultural activities (second order functions) were originally believed to be rooted in the experience of sexual activity and, even more basically, of bipolar relationship—that traditionally, therefore, a human being could not be a full participant in his or her community *in terms of socio-cultural activity* unless he 'died' to the unitary rhythm of childhood's self-expression and was 'reborn' at the level of duality and sexual relatedness.

The very widespread practice of circumcision—now being

mostly performed for purely materialistic or health reasons—
had an eminently ritualistic meaning. When, as was usually the
case (except among the Jewish people), it occurred at the time
of puberty, it symbolized a thorough and unhindered opening
to the power of 'life' in its bipolar sexual aspect—an opening
required for participation in socio-cultural process, which at the
tribal level were entirely based on life-energy. The ceremony
was mythically performed by frightening divine Beings, because
culture was then purely the deification or sacralized extension of
natural life-processes—an extension involving the triumph over
the fatality of body-death, thanks to the transmission of collectively acquired knowledge from one generation to the next.

The Hebraic practice of circumcision a few days after birth
symbolically refers to the belief in and worship of the one and
only God—who is the god of life, ruler of the biosphere. The
Jewish child is consecrated to this one God by circumcision at
the beginning of his development as a human being. The boy is
immediately made a *potential* participant in 'the people'. He is
also thereby prepared to later on take the new step which,
through the use of intellect-power, will open to him the realm of
functions of the third order and especially accelerate and
strengthen the development of his ego. The fact that female
infants were not circumcised is quite revealing of the ritualistic
association of the 'sacred' with maleness. This is the patriarchal
tradition; it leaves to the woman a most basic role in the realm
of the 'profane', especially as ruler of the home and biological
processes.

This has also been the case in Christendom; but the Church
does baptize and give communion and confirmation *equally* to
boys and girls. Behind this difference between the Hebrew and
Catholic traditions stands the fact that in Hebrew culture there
is no basic opposition between the realms of religion and social
processes—the two realms are essentially inseparable—whereas
Christianity sharply differentiates the activities belonging to
"Caesar" from those belonging to "God" (or Christ). Yet, even
according to the Christian tradition, a castrated man cannot
become a priest, because priesthood implies an ascetic overcoming of the 'passions of the flesh', and there is no overcoming

when there is nothing to overcome. The patriarchal attitude is also retained in the exclusion of women from priesthood, but this may have been due to the influence of the Hebrew tradition which, through the strong personality of Paul, deeply affected many aspects of the Christian doctrines.

One could develop the relation between sex and socio-cultural activities at great length; but all that is needed in this psychological study is to understand how sex operates as a function of transition between strictly biological and socio-cultural processes. Life, through sex, develops into culture. With sex, problems of bipolar relationship appear; these in turn soon give rise to group tensions and the possibility of many-sided relationships and violent conflicts. This possibility has to be controlled if the human species is to survive. Built-in controls develop, that are *both* 'sanctioned' or 'sacralized' by religion and externalized in attractive forms (thus, glorified) by rituals and special objects symbolizing either the deeper aspect of the bipolar relationship or the action of superior Beings—or of God—made to participate in it. The most common of such rituals is the marriage ceremony.

Each culture has given to this ceremony its own particular form, and a discussion of the symbolism inherent in the many marriage rituals of the past and the present cannot be attempted here. What many people in our culture seem to forget is that until very recently marriage had very little to do with the personal likes and emotional feelings of two individuals consciously choosing to unite their lives for joint self-fulfillment. In most cases, marriage had essentially, and often exclusively, only two functions. One was more strictly biological—the perpetuation of the distinctive genetic character of a particular race or national combination of racial types through the production of children. The other was more typically socio-cultural, as it referred to the perpetuation of a particular socio-cultural way of life and a religious tradition, as these were understood and practiced by a particular group or class of people.

In the Western world, the traditional marriage ceremony actually involves *four* participants: the bride and bridegroom, society (represented by the parents and the priest) and God. Any sexual union not including the last two has for centuries been considered 'sinful', even though in some cases tolerated as a marginal and extrasocial form of activity. For a man and woman of different cultural and/or religious backgrounds to marry was considered outrageous and could not be sanctified by a religious ritual. Only a civil marriage was possible, and even those were not acceptable in all societies. The color barrier was, of course, often totally impassable, even at the civil level—in principle so as to preserve the purity of racial characteristics. It is only when (at least in theory) the functions of the third order begin to dominate the collective mentality of a people that marriage begins to be accepted as the conscious, deliberate, and relatively open union of two 'individuals'. But the inertial power of customs and dominant institutions is so great that marriage until very recently had to retain its biological-cultural character. It is only within the last hundred years that the third factor in the marriage ritual—society and the parents—has taken a secondary place in a growing number of instances. As to the fourth factor (God), it is now most often ignored, or in some cases is replaced by the instinctual or impersonalized feeling of communion or attunement to vitalistic or even cosmic energies— energies which once had been personalized as gods in 'pagan' religions.

b. *The Discursive Intellect and the Process of Individualization*

The process of 'liberation' from the concrete, instinctual mind, operating as a servant of 'life', requires the development of an analytical and discursive type of thought process to which we refer today when speaking of the *intellect*. This intellect becomes a powerful tool through which man's consciousness is able objectively and unemotionally to look at all existential changes in himself as well as in the world. But more than that, it is glorified as the great liberator through rigidly controlled analytical techniques, such as the Socratic method of 'discourse', pro-and-con arguments and dialectics.

When seen in its analytical and discursive aspect, the intellect can be considered the function of transition between the second and third orders of function, because it represents the most advanced development along the line of socio-cultural relatedness and of what Korzybsky called the "time binding faculty" in man. By separating its objectivized perceptions from the concrete and ephemeral reality of the biopsychic world—which is the foundation of all other cultural processes—the human intellect is able to deal with relations and concepts unaffected by changes produced by the flow of time and, thus with universal 'constants' and deterministic (because rationalistic) 'laws of nature'. At least in principle, this intellect is not affected by emotions arising from biological, psychic, and socio-political pressures and impacts. Moreover, the knowledge derived from intellectual processes is easily communicable and translatable in diverse languages. It spans generations as well as continents.

However, the development of the intellectual function is a Pandora's box which, when opened, releases a vast series of consequences. Intellectual knowledge presupposes a *knower,* objective to what is being known; it requires knowers whose mental activity is not affected by biopsychic pressures and directives—thus who have become free from the compulsions of their biospheric nature, at least in some areas of their consciousness. These knowers, if they are to obtain a truly 'universal' kind of knowledge, have to be free, not only from the energies of 'life', but also from the limiting and particular assumptions characterizing any culture and the social and political pressures of society.

Because it is the foundation on which functions of the third order develop, the intellect has to be at least relatively separate from, and unmoved by, the activities of the first (biological) and second (socio-cultural) orders. It has to become 'individualized' and autonomous if it is to function in terms of pure reason. The discursive mind analyzes what the senses perceive, what the organism-as-a-whole (and its organic parts) feels, what the collective tradition presents as revealed truth, and the challenge of knowledge *per se.* To analyze is to break away from the feeling of wholeness and empathy. It is to atomize what the collective will and consciousness (society) forcefully presented as 'reality' and common sense in the realm where personal and group security are far more important than objective facts. Only individuals able to stand apart from and, to some extent at first, against the collective mentality of their culture and tradition may effectively perform such a catabolic task.

This separative and atomizing activity of the intellectual aspect of the mind is a necessary phase in the process of human evolution; just as, in logic, the antithesis is an integral part of a syllogism leading from the thesis to the synthesis. But this atomistic and discursive intellect should be considered as only a transitory stage between the compulsive biopsychic activity of the archaic, relatively unconscious, and essentially collective mind, and the individually conscious, yet also holistic and unanimistic activity of the 'supermind' within which all human consciousnesses *potentially* interpenetrate.

Similarly, the individualizing 'I-feeling' should be regarded as only a transitory experience on which an antithetic kind of mentality and world-view—pluralistic, atomistic or 'monadistic', and in socio-political terms, 'democratic'—can be legitimately based, and for a time, *should be* based.

To say this, however, is to consider only one aspect of the situation created by the emergence and stabilization of the consciousness of being a distinct individual person no longer totally dominated by biological and cultural compulsions. What this consciousness means and implies is not always clearly understood, whether at the metaphysical level or in terms of practical and concrete psychological realizations. I have discussed this complex and often all-too-emotionally-approached subject in several books, particularly in *The Planetarization of Consciousness*, and I shall only mention here, and in the last chapter, some points particularly relevant to the psychological approach I am now taking.

Individualization is based on the ability inherent in human beings to refer their sensations, perceptions, and organismic or psychic feelings to a center. It seems quite evident that the centralizing of human experience is a relatively late factor in the evolution of human consciousness. For a long time during the archaic ages, human beings experienced existential changes in an unfocalized manner. These changes were felt to take place in a field of happenings having no well-defined rhythm, boundaries, or center. When the feeling of 'center' arose, it was referred to the community as a whole. It had a collective character. It was projected outwardly as the god of the tribe. This god ruled the whole tribe and the world in which it collectively operated. He was the creator and the all-powerful center of the tribal world whose physical center was the village plaza.

As the field of tribal activity extended and became a vast empire or kingdom, reliance on the tribal god as a center of power and guidance became superseded by the worship of a universal God Who centralized and ruled over a multiplicity of lesser gods and spirits—just as the deified Persian emperor, Darius, ruled over many smaller nations and tribes through an administrative bureaucracy and provincial sub-rulers.

When Jesus taught the revolutionary doctrine that the Kingdom of Heaven is *within* every human being, he was saying that what was once considered the structuring power of the universe should actually be experienced at the core of any person's being as the 'Inner Ruler'. He also spoke of "our Father who art in Heaven," thus seemingly suggesting what had been taught in a different manner in India since Sri Krishna and the Upanishads —that is, the identity of the universal Center and the centers in all individuals.

In India the revelatory realization that the universal *brahman* and the individual *atman* are essentially one remained a central factor in all Hindu philosophies, each of which was thought to provide a particular way of experiencing this mystical identity— each way being valid for the particular type of human beings whose stage in spiritual evolution required this special approach. But in the Western world, the social manifestation of this ideal of identity was overwhelmed by a traditional subservience to a central authority—a tradition, which, as we shall see later on, began in its present form after Cyrus founded the Persian empire in the sixth century b. c. Our Euro-American society inherited this tradition from Imperial Rome which, consciously and unconsciously, had absorbed the Persian and the late Egyptian models.

As a result, a dualistic situation was established in the collective mind of our Western world, such a dualism being symbolized by the two most powerful symbolic images of our culture, Caesar and Christ. It led to a division between the socio-political and the spiritual-individual spheres. In the latter sphere, God was worshipped as the universal Center, transcendent to the contents of the cosmic field of existence; but at the same time, every human being was understood to have within himself, as an ideal, *the archetypal image* of this divine centrality. By actualizing *this potential form of existence,* he or she would partake of the nature of the Deity—even though there could be no question of actual 'identification', the Creator and His creatures remaining forever and essentially distinct. Man could become 'unified', but never 'identified', with a God that was conceived to be essentially external to the cosmos, just as an artist is external to his creations, even if involved in them and in what will become of them when they leave his studio.

If man is created in the image and likeness of such a God, logically, he too has to be essentially external to his small world, of which he is, if not strictly speaking the creator, at least the interpreter and namer. For the rather mysterious purpose of learning some lesson, man is thought to exist on an Earth to which, as a God-created soul, he does not really belong. The Earth is not his true 'home', only a 'school'. But when involved in the activities of the terrestrial environment, he almost inevitably becomes fascinated by and addicted to the energies and passions of 'this world'. He becomes its prisoner, and his main task is to *detach* his consciousness from its allurements. Seen at the emotional level, this detachment is called 'severance'; at the level of mind, it is 'ab-straction'. At every level, man has to overcome the pull of the whorls of life-energies.

In the process of abstraction, the human mind must detach and separate itself from what it observes, analyzes, and eventually transforms. The mind *detaches* certain basic features (or some apparently essential relationships) from the direct and total experience of reality, and as a result, a geometrical or conceptual pattern takes form within the consciousness. In a direct life-experience, the entire organism reacts to a whole situation; however, at the biological level of consciousness, the reaction is instinctual and while some type of consciousness is involved, it is a *generic* type which—in terms of what we generally think of today as consciousness—is actually subconscious. At the socio-cultural level, the members of the tribal or post-tribal society essentially react to situations according to patterns of feeling, thinking, and behavior which have been forcibly impressed upon their minds by the language, the behavior, and the teachings of the community, and these reactions leave out whatever, in the whole situation, is unacceptable to the tradition. Consciousness has essentially a *collective* character.

At about the time when the collective mentality of a culture-whole reaches a point at which the capacity for abstraction takes a significant importance—at least in the thinking processes of a 'creative minority'—the process of individualization at the feeling-level has progressed to the stage at which the experience of 'being I' becomes not only fully conscious, but mentalized. It centers the field of consciousness not merely in a semi-instinctive organic sense ("I want this," "This is mine," "I am different"), but as a foundation for an overall metaphysical principle inherent in the concept of 'being'. 'I' becomes an abstraction, separated and detached from body experiences and emotional feelings. Individualism develops as a social principle of action expressing what is now regarded as the essential reality of the universe, that is, the existence of a multiplicity of abstract-transcendental units of being. These units may be called God-created immortal Souls, monads, or *jivas* (in Jain philosophy). They are ab-stracted from the *indivisible wholeness* of the universal Whole.

The concept of an absolute individuality, featured in some Western and even Eastern metaphysics (for instance in the philosophy of 'Personalism'), is an abstraction; and it should be clearly differentiated from the biological feeling of organic wholeness based on the fact that the organism actually is a structured field of interrelated and interdependent functional activities. This concept differs also from the ego which develops as a response of the organism-as-a-whole to the pressures of family and society.

One might say that the concept of absolute individuality is

like that of a center without a circumference. One cannot logically speak of a center without conceiving a circle and circumference, just as one should not speak of a father or mother without a child, or at least a child-in-the-making. Any 'point' theoretically can become a center, but it is only *potentially* so until
its surrounding space has been filled and organized as a field of
radiation around it.

In a similar sense, making of a moment of time an absolute
concept and glorifying it as the 'Now' implies that a particular
moment—theoretically any particular moment—is being ab-
stracted from the human experience of the ever-flowing process
of universal change and given an absolute meaning. This is
done, and a particular person is conceptually taken out (ab-
stracted) from his planetary environment (and ultimately from
the cosmos as a whole), when it becomes important to transfer
the focus of human consciousness, feelings, and attention from
the biological and cultural levels of functions of the first and
second order to that of functions of the fourth order. When the
consciousness of man *has to* be gradually detached from biology
and a local and exclusivistic culture—because the time for such
a change of focus and level has come in the planetary process
of human evolution—*then* the crisis of individualization and
severance from the biocultural past expresses itself as a glorification of the individual-in-itself and the moment-in-itself. *'Now'*
detachment becomes imperative. The crucial choice, the Day of
Judgement, has come. One must go through the transition process
leading to a yet-unknown state of spiritual being, or fall by the
wayside and return to the condition of undifferentiated matter.

This transition process *makes use* of the mental faculties and
the innate feeling of order that biology and culture have built,
but these faculties are used in a manner that actually destroys
their biocultural foundations. Similarly, when the seed forms
within the fruit, the plant begins to die. The seed 'kills' the
plant; but in time the seed also will germinate and die into the
new plant. Biological and cultural values lose their potency and
focalized meaning, transferring these to the glorified individual
who, as independent and self-determined world citizen, detached

from family, national, and cultural localisms, is theoretically free, ready and able to join with other individuals of different or similar backgrounds in the building of a new transcultural and thus universal society.

The entire development of culture-wholes leads toward just such a period of prolonged crisis during which the functions of the third order acquire an often exaggerated importance and the process of abstraction and conceptualization may tend to run wild in intellectual minds losing touch with holistic life-experiences and planetary realities. Individuals, in their emotional eagerness to become 'liberated' from the domination of all that a culture imposes upon them—or in rarer cases, from the compulsive power of the nutritive and sexual functions, and in general from any desire related to the physical body—easily forget that every individual person is but one of billions of variations on the theme, Man. Each individualized person draws out of this theme and seeks to significantly express and realize one, but only *one*, of its latent potentialities, just as every culture-whole constitutes but one kind of matrix to enwomb the eventual development of independent, totally conscious, inwardly free, and emotionally unattached individuals.

In a very broad sense, the development of any culture-whole resembles the gestation of an embryo within a mother-womb. Alas, if we follow this analogy, the vast majority of pregnancies are miscarriages, or more accurately, there are only an extremely few seeds covering the forest's soil in the fall which become trees, or a very few fish eggs in the ocean that will experience a full adult development. Yet nothing is wasted and the chemicals contained in the trillions of non-germinating seeds give to the humus substances that will significantly contribute to the few germinating seeds. This is the great lesson, so hard for human beings to learn: the lesson of sacrifice and *service*.

Every living organism serves a planetary, and ultimately a cosmic, purpose. Only a few are able, through a process of *self-consecration*, to emerge as positive and creative factors at the level of the functions of the fourth order. The number of such men and women today is fast increasing, because the evolu-

tionary crisis of mankind appears relatively imminent, and the
pressure for conscious, deliberate, and courageous, if not heroic,
decisions is steady and irrepressible.

c. *Consecrating the Self to the Whole*

A time comes during the process of development of the individualized consciousness when the human being who has striven
so long after the satisfaction and aggrandizement of his ruling
ego is compelled by sheer self-interest to learn to cooperate with
other egos for the achievement of some common purpose. Cooperation in action is the foundation of socio-cultural activities,
but at the early tribal level of society, and in the traditional
family situation—which today often appears to be a thing of
the historical past—the need to cooperate is instinctually recognized and unquestioned. It is based on a nearly compulsive
sense of group-identification. The unity of the whole takes an
uncontrovertible precedence over the desires and the opinions of
individual members.

As a society becomes increasingly complex, especially in large
cities, the 'citizen' acts primarily as an ego, even if not self-
sufficient and self-motivated, at least claiming loudly and
proudly the right to "do his own thing" regardless of the consequences to others and especially to the whole. When the value
of cooperation takes hold of the consciousness, it presents itself
to the ego-consciousness as self-interest. This is the underlying
principle of 'democracy'. Individuals join together *in order to*
achieve the much publicized purposes mentioned in the Preamble
of the U. S. Constitution; they join strictly, or rather theoretically, as 'individual persons' whose individuality not only has
'worth and dignity' but is given in principle a quasi-absolute
value—even if there are a great many instances when practice
contradicts principle.

Even at the supposedly more idealistic level of ethics, people
are enjoined to be 'good' *in order to* reach Heaven after death,
or gain good Karma and be reborn in a high caste family, or
simply because it supposedly pays to be good—in one form

or another—while the opposite way of acting does not. What is considered optimal well-being at the biological level becomes personal happiness in societies in which the process of individualization has been not only operative, but glorified and sanctioned by philosophers and theologists worshipping an equally 'personal' God.

When cooperation and 'being good' are no longer matters of so-called free choice made by the ego, but have instead become an ineradicable part of the nature of an individual, one can say that the transition to the fourth order of functions has begun. When a man can decide not to do an evil act and perhaps some kind of pro and con argument about the matter occurs within his mind, this man is only 'good'. The person who operates *fully* at the level of functions of the fourth order *cannot* choose evil; there can be in him no inner pro and con argument, no private discourse about the value of goodness. His essential nature makes it impossible for him to act in any other way. He is no longer 'free' to be either good or bad. He is totally and unquestionably what he is; that is, he is irrevocably *self-consecrated* to the whole of which he *knows* himself indubitably to be an operative aspect or quality.

This kind of knowing is intellectually irrefutable because it is an inner fact of existence beyond intellectual as well as moral alternatives. We may call it 'intuition', just as we may call 'compassion' the type of realization through which a person feels so intimately one with all other persons (or even all other living entities), that the 'gift-waves' of an impersonal (or rather, transpersonal) love flows from him or her toward whoever needs such a power of compassionate Christ-love. There are evidently degrees of intensity in the development of this intuition and compassion; their actual operative field may be restricted or vast, yet the principle of self-consecration by an individual to the whole can be active whether the field is relatively narrow—because the person's experience is limited by physical conditions—or planetary in scope. Yet if there really is self-consecration of the individual to the whole, there first of all needs to be an 'individual'—a conscious, self-motivated person who has experienced the dilemmas created by freedom of choice in the past, and now has reached beyond them in the lucidity and inner certainty of transpersonal consciousness and spiritual being.

The word 'consecration' should be clearly understood. When an object is to be used by a priest, or any kind of officiant in a religious or magical ritual, and it is 'con-secrated', it is transferred from the level of the 'profane' to that of the 'sacred'. It is brought ceremonially—thus, with the assent or cooperation of a group of people—into the category or realm of what inherently possesses the character of the sacred.

In his book, *The Sacred and the Profane,* Mircea Eliade clearly shows that for the archaic mentality, the quality of sacredness belongs to the actions of the gods, as they set in motion the world as a whole, or at least a particular cycle of existence. The time of creation is a special kind of time which, in a sense, does not pass away. It remains always 'now'; and the purpose of sacred ceremonies is to re-attune the community to the quality of that original moment when a god creates.

Extending this concept or this feeling of awe and mystery when confronted by any creative act—creative because it initiates a totally new cycle of existence—we can see how any period of transition from one realm of being (or one level of consciousness) to the next is to be seen as the preparation for a sacred moment at which the new cycle or the new life is born. In the process of individual development, this period or preparation takes the form of 'the Path' that leads to Initiation. The disciple on that Path is being prepared to be a potentially sacred vessel or instrumentality into which a superpersonal power will become focused at the sacred moment of Initiation. In that moment, the disciple becomes 'con-secrated' by the Hierophant, priest, or medicine-man, and accepted as such by the community of those who have already become sacred. He becomes a participant in the field of activity of a larger whole.

This process of consecration can occur at any level; and there are levels upon levels of initiation. Any initiation, in the commonly used sense of the term, implies an initiator. As already stated, in archaic times, a true and major initiation in the occult-planetary sense represented the transfer of the power of an 'office' (an occult planetary function) from the initiator to his disciple, the disciple thereafter replacing the former who had bequeathed to him the power of the office. In more recent times—perhaps since the Buddha or the Christ—it now seems possible for human beings to consciously and deliberately generate the power to actualize in a self-determined and self-induced, yet natural, manner what for long ages had been in man only the potentiality of superpersonal and spiritual consciousness and activity. In this sense, it has become possible to consecrate oneself *as an individual* to a consciously recognized and at least partially understood super-individual kind of existence. I might over-simplify the matter by saying that in the past, it was the member of a guiding Hierarchy of spiritual planetary Beings who selected and tested his potential disciple for a definite 'functional' purpose, while during the last two millennia, it has been possible for any human being to develop as a self-motivated individual to the point at which he or she is impelled by an inner necessity of growth to seek a Teacher or spiritual Guide who may assist in the preparatory steps toward effective self-consecration. And self-consecration—in terms of the psychology of operative wholeness being outlined in this book—essentially implies an inner readiness and indeed a commitment to develop the functions of the fourth order through a process of 'ego-surrender' or rather, ego-metamorphosis.

Inner readiness and commitment, however, only constitute the first phase of a process which quite evidently is not completed until there has been a definite acceptance of the aspirant as a full-fledged member of the Spiritual Community of Man. Such a community should be understood as the perfect collective product of mankind's evolution. It represents *the omega condition* of the development of human consciousness and human society operative at a level of supremely conscious and differentiated unanimity (or 'multi-unity'). At this transphysical level, interpenetration has taken the place of separation, and the individual is so totally the servant of the whole that he has lost all sense of egocentricity.

The principle of individual selfhood implies that of centrality, and centrality in turn implies a circumference. The French philosopher Pascal (perhaps unconsciously repeating what had been said before him in the East) defined God as the circle whose center is everywhere and circumference nowhere. This refers to what I have called the Pleroma state in which every unit-center is the whole, and the whole operates totally in every center. It is the state of perfect *plenitude of being*. We can think of such a state in an all-encompassing 'pancosmic' sense and call it God, but we should also realize that it can be understood to exist *in a relative sense* as the end-culmination of any large cycle of existence, especially at a planetary—and therefore all-human—level. It is all-human because, I repeat, Man is the conscious mind of the planet, Earth. As we know him today, Man is mind conscious of being conscious, because centralized in the experience of 'I am'. But Man is still in the making. Having reached the level of functions of the third order (which by blending with those of the first and second orders has deeply transformed them, mankind is now reaching a symbolical 'change of life' through which it becomes *possible* to develop, in a collective and publicly accepted manner, functions of the fourth order.

But this is only a possibility. It might not be actualized at this time, for an enormous majority of human beings today seem still unready and, indeed, incapable of consciously and effectively taking the great step of self-consecration to the whole of humanity. However, the present-day crisis offers an unparalleled opportunity for a 'creative minority' to rise from the disintegrating or inchoate masses and take their stand. Today, it is a private concern—or at best, a group decision, provided the group is a group of truly individualized, self-determined and responsible individuals, and not merely an aggregation of more or less fashion-influenced or emotionally distraught and egocentric personalities. But, who can tell what tomorrow might bring, particularly if we should have to face a planetary catharsis directly affecting every human being in body, mind and soul?

The important thing at this critical point in the evolution of mankind and of each of the millennial cultures that control the masses of men, women, and children, is for philosophers and psychologists—and last, but not least, religious and political leaders jealously entrenched in age-old privileges—to become aware of new possibilities. The important thing is to be open to the acceptance of the supernormal, even if mixed with the abnormal. Such an openness should certainly retain its ability to discriminate, but it has to forego the desire or habit—characteristic in our Western culture—to fragment, atomize and analyze away what can only be understood as the structured development of an organic whole.

I have already spoken of the holistic mind, the mind able to see and encompass any situation or living organism as a whole of interdependent functional activities, and (as I defined the term) as a 'cosmos'—whether it be a microcosm or macrocosm, an atom, a human person, a solar system, or a galaxy. To so 'cosmify' existence in all its aspects, even the most menial, is to make use of the 'cosmogenic' function. It is also to *sacralize* all existential activities, and to transform the performance of all our functions in everyday social living into sacraments.

The sacralization of existence, if properly understood, takes a new character at the level of functions of the fourth order, because it is no longer—or at least not exclusively—referred to a divine Creation considered as the one sacred Act of God or gods; it is seen as the essential prerogative of mankind acting collectively and unanimously toward the full planetary actualization of the *precosmic* potential that the original divine Creation actualized *only in germ*. It is this 'germinal' Act that the creative gods performed. But prior to this germ and the rootlet that gave power to this rising tender germ was the seed. The seed is pure potentiality. The germ, from which roots and stem develop, is the beginning of the process of actualization of the seed-potentiality of existence.

In the Theosophical symbolism formulated for the nineteenth century mentality by H. P. Blavatsky in *The Secret Doctrine*, mention is made of a Root-Manu and a Seed-Manu. The concept of the *Manu* has been popularized and personified both in the Hindu tradition and the works of latter-day Theosophists; but H. P. Blavatsky makes it clear that Manu is meant to be, in one sense, the Archetypal Pattern (or divine Form) of an entire cycle of human development (to which the today emotionally confusing term 'Race' is given), and in another sense, the collectivity of the spiritual entities that will ensoul and incarnate into the human bodies operating during that cycle.

In terms of the functions of first and second orders (biology and culture), 'the sacred' occurred in the past—even though this past may, in a deeper spiritual sense, always be present and 'ever-young' during a large cycle of existence. In contrast (for the consciousness inherent in functions of the fourth order), 'the sacred' is a process leading to a future in-the-making; and this future is Man-the-Seed, the global Community of Perfected Men. It is this *in-the-making* which is the sacred performance. The process itself—the whole of existence—is thus felt and visualized as a multifarious sacrament. The spiritual life is a life of consecrated selfhood realized in the sacramental perform-ance of every activity—human, subhuman or transhuman. For the individual person, the goal of such an existence is—through the ever-repeated act of self-consecration to the Whole—the full development of the cosmogenic function, with its twin foun-dations of intuition (holistic mind) and compassion (Christic love). For any human collectivity and for mankind as a whole (once organized and having planetary consciousness), the one sacred goal is the development of the Pleroma of Perfected Human Beings—the omega state of planetary fulfillment, the "Seed Manu".

This is the ultimate goal of the planetary cycle of Man. It may, indeed, seem incredibly remote and its actualization nearly impossible. But this future *is now being made*. It is being made in every victory over the inertia of bodily automatism, of so-cio-cultural institutions and bureaucratic organizations, and of self-complacent and too often ambitious, greedy, and violence-prone egos; for we must not forget that the functions of the fourth order develop on the basis of functions of the first, sec-ond and third orders—that is, on the basis of biology, culture, and individuality.

Today all orders of function operate—or at least *can* operate—at once. They are all interdependent; each affects all, at least to some extent. The future seed is already implied in the tender vernal germ, even though the old seed yet remains, partially feeding the new growth. The leaves long for the flower; and the core of the flower is haloed by the latent image of the seed maturing within the growing protection of the fruit. The whole process of existence is sacred, once the holistic mind is able to perceive it as a beautiful performance. Beauty resides only in the whole. There is no integrity, no harmony, no peace except in the whole. To that wholeness, may all individuals consecrate themselves in the heroic performance of their own function, at their own place—their unique and sacred *dharma*.

Part Two

The Collective-Social Mode

4

FROM BIOLOGY TO CULTURE

Because of the intensive specialization characterizing our present-day type of knowledge, psychology on the one hand, and anthropology and archaeology on the other, are considered very different fields of study. Nevertheless, it has become quite clear to some psychologists that the character and development of an individual person cannot be fully understood unless they are referred to his social and even geographical environment, and that one should speak of the individual-in-his-environment rather than consider the individual as a 'thing-in-itself'. Thus a field of study is developing, *psychosociology,* in which the complex interaction between the individual and the collective is a basic factor.

Societies are born, mature, and disintegrate much as individual persons do, and the enormous wealth of material collected and integrated by philosopher-historians like Oswald Spengler and Arnold Toynbee give a seemingly solid foundation to the belief —nevertheless unacceptable to most historians clinging to a purely empirical method—that societies, or what I call culture-wholes, can indeed be considered as organized systems of interrelated and interdependent activities closely associated with particular geographical regions and developing certain characteristic features giving them the character of organisms—if the term 'organism' is used in the broad sense I give to it.

If a society (or culture-whole) can be considered a 'collective personality'—and modern nations certainly display features similar to those characterizing individual persons—the obvious next step is to consider them as units operating, both simultaneously and successively, within a larger whole—mankind. And as mankind functions within a circumscribed environment, the biosphere of the Earth, we have to think of human societies as components of a planetary system of interrelated activities. Sociology, history (as one usually understands this term), and anthropology should therefore be considered parts of an integral study dealing with the global evolution of humanity in relation to the development of the planet Earth.

The difficulty this approach meets is that the data available for such a study are most insufficient and controversial. They are made controversial for two reasons. Modern science accepts only physical evidence as the source of valid data and dismisses archaic traditions and 'myths' as imaginative fairy-tales produced by a child-like mentality projecting its needs, its fears or hopes, and its fantasies upon non-physical realms to which our now mature and rational minds should no longer attribute the character of 'reality'. On the other hand, the factual discoveries of anthropologists and archaeologists are in most instances so fragmentary and leave so many basic questions unanswered that they are susceptible to many interpretations and indeed are often re-evaluated. Geological data are also still quite uncertain, as differences of opinion prevail concerning the character of the forces at work on our planet in very ancient times and the speed at which geological changes—such as the shifting, appearance and disappearance of continents—have occurred.

In spite of all this uncertainty, it seems very important for us, especially today in a period of potentially crucial all-human and perhaps telluric transformation, to develop a broad, holistic, and truly planetary approach to the evolution of mankind. This implies looking at the main widely-disseminated concepts with an open mind.

a. *Mythic and Materialistic Approaches*

What we might call the traditional-mythological picture of the origin and development of civilization has been scorned by Western intellectuals, but it has recently taken the form which appeals to many people, even among the most educated classes. In its occult aspect, this picture was formulated a century ago by H P Blavatsky in the second volume (Anthropogenesis) of

The Secret Doctrine, and a number of other writers (especially Rudolf Steiner) have developed some aspects of it. It is based on a cosmic view of the entire process of existence, from the very beginning of the universe and of life on this Earth. It implies the activity of spiritual-cosmic forces and entities at the source of the development of mankind—an activity which has never ceased and which in archaic times manifested as the rule of a higher type of human beings (Divine Kings and Teachers of agriculture and the arts) who aided the evolution of the undeveloped masses of humanity.

Today the possibility that in the distant past higher beings from other planets or solar systems were instrumental in bringing to an animal-like humanity the rudiments of civilization has been highly publicized by books and motion pictures. Very ancient, unexplained constructions and various records all over the world have at times been convincingly interpreted as the vestiges of presumably advanced cultures developed by a few powerful extraterrestrial entities in more or less human form to whom a divine character and origin was attributed by the masses. Besides, the shape of the floor of the Atlantic Ocean and of the continents on either side of it no doubt suggests the possibility of the existence of a vast super-continent including much of the Americas, Africa and parts of Europe and having gradually broken into two parts. This division could then be related to the 'myth' of Atlantis, and to the struggle between two ways of life—so called 'white' and 'black' magicians—fighting for supremacy. There may have been a catastrophe near Crete in the Mediterranean during the second millennium B. C., but if so, this cataclysmic volcanic explosion was a much later event. Distant memories often become blended in archaic traditions, because for the archaic mind the *meaning* of events and the nature of the shock they produce in the collective psyche of the people are far more important than the events themselves objectively considered.

The other main approach to man's evolution may be called Darwinian and materialistic because it takes for granted that no factors other than man's adaptation to his material environment and the effect of the struggle for life operate in the process leading from primitive ape-like men in a condition of so-called 'barbarism' to what we still like to extol as 'civilization'. The nineteenth century idea of straightforward linear progress has lost much of its credibility since our two World Wars and the widespread use of physical and/or mental torture by governments; yet very few academic thinkers, historians, and archaeologists are ready to give up their *a priori* belief that in the archaic ages *only* primitive human beings existed on this Earth. Nevertheless, even if we were to assume that there is no remaining physical evidence of far distant civilizations or of dynasties of 'divine' Kings of superhuman or extraterrestrial origin, it is quite easy to see how all records of such beings could have been obliterated, covered by sands and jungles or submerged. If a planet-wide catastrophe would sink most of the now-populated land and leave only some sections of undeveloped regions inhabited by heavily traumatized communities, most of what is left of our modern civilization some hundreds of thousands of years hence could well have been forgotten, or vaguely remembered as the mythical existence of extraordinary beings.

However, the point I wish to make here is not that there actually were such aristocracies of superior beings (of whatever origin), but that the possibility of their existence should not be dismissed *a priori*, especially as this existence would solve many riddles. Any valid scientific theory should account for *all* the facts and leave no mystery; and psychological mysteries are as much to be taken into account as physical ones. Moreover, the existence of superior beings on the planet in no way eliminates the slow process of evolution affecting *the masses* of mankind. It does not invalidate the natural and normal development of human functions from the compulsive, biological, and tribal state to that of the ideal 'Holy City' that would mark the ultimate transphysical condition of human development on this Earth. In any case, the biopsychical activities of human beings remain *the foundation* upon which the development of 'higher' functions rests; and the process of individualization is still basic as the necessary means to achieve full and objective consciousness; and this process requires the existence of culture-wholes as matrices for the rise of individuals.

If there once were superior quasi-divine beings on Earth as

Teachers and Rulers of *some* (but most likely not all) tribes of men, these superior beings are *not* to be considered 'individuals' in our sense of the term. We should think of them as 'seed beings' from some other planet or evolutionary scheme. The Bible refers to them in Genesis (Chapter 6) as the *Ben Elohim*, the Sons of the Creative Gods (*Elohim* is a *plural* noun) who "married the daughters of men." The result of the process—whatever it entailed—apparently did not have good results, and a world cataclysm ensued. A new humanity may have developed out of a *remnant*, but even if this remnant (or 'seed group') was composed of the most perfect human beings the old civilization had produced, these men may not have been the *only* humans left on the globe. If such a cataclysm did occur, some countries were probably not affected greatly. In these lands, scattered tribes may have been operating at a very primitive and strictly biological level of evolution—many such tribes still existed on our present globe during our Industrial and Technological Revolutions!—and it would have been to these tribes that the 'seed men' taught agriculture and the use of all the functions of the second order.

The difficulty which the modern mind has in accepting such a historical 'model' of mankind's development lies in the prejudice our Western intellectuals have against accepting the possibility of *simultaneous* existence on our planet of human beings of basically different origins and levels of development. Yet there would be no such difficulty if we could think of mankind as a complex whole—a field of functional activities operating at several levels and within a still larger planetary organism, the Earth. This whole, mankind, develops gradually according to definite patterns. This development—of which what we call 'history' is only a very small part—follows an identifiable rhythm and has a number of successive phases. Each culture-whole is related to one of these phases, and therefore occupies a definite position within the entire evolutionary process. It has a specific function to perform; and the performance may be either adequate or inadequate. It may end in some kind of catastrophe, necessitating a radical readjustment; but it is conceivable that, as an important phase of the evolutionary process ends, the concluding period is to some degree always catastrophic (or let us

say, catabolic), destructive operations having become necessary
to offset cultural and institutional inertia. This may not be so
when the change from one phase of the evolutionary process to
the next is not so radical as to completely upset the balance of
power of the forces operating in the socio-cultural field. Yet every
phase constitutes a small cyclic development having a more or less
clear-cut beginning and end, and at every end, some kind of
transfer of power and consciousness can be seen involving some
type of relatively violent and/or destructive activity.

When we consider the development of a culture-whole—as
Arnold Toynbee described such a process, for instance—we find
that this development ends with the transfer of power from a
disintegrating society to a more primitive, yet intensely dynamic,
race or group of tribes; but the old society has also produced
some kind of 'spiritual harvest' which becomes incorporated in
a universal religion that in time will mold the consciousness and
affect the behavior of the conquerors as well as the disintegrated
remains of the old society. The individual human beings who
are, as it were, the carriers of this spiritual harvest are the 'seed
men' of the vanishing culture-whole. In relation to the morally
and culturally deteriorated masses of people still representing
the dying past but surviving through the chaotic centuries or
decades marking the transition from one culture-whole to the
next, and even more, perhaps, in relation to the rough and un-
cultivated 'barbarians' who will form the dominant substance of
the new society, these seed men represent a superior type of
mind. Thus at such a time of transition, we find different levels
of mental activity embodied in human persons of different type
and origin coexisting and cooperating.

This is *historically* evident during the period of breakdown
of the Roman Empire and while the Medieval European culture-
whole was emerging out of the ruins and the chaos of the 'Dark
Ages'. A similar process, but at a far deeper and more cosmic
level, has been *mythologically* described in the Sacred Scriptures
and the traditional poetry of nearly all peoples of the world in
terms of the existence upon the Earth of 'divine' beings who
revealed to a very primitive humanity the foundations of culture—that is, they aroused in men the ability to act, become
related, and think in terms of functions of the second order. The

existence of such beings should present no problem to minds able to think in terms of principles of cyclic and cosmic evolution, provided—I repeat—they understand that these beings are *not* to be considered as 'individuals' in our present sense of the term. Whatever their origin was, they must have represented fields of activity operating at a level similar to what I have called the fourth order of functions. They must have been 'cosmic' minds.

What this means should be clear if we accept at least the possibility that human evolution operates according to a 'dialectical' rhythm—thesis, antithesis and synthesis—to which I have already referred (cf. p. 17). The most important point to consider in terms of such a sequence is that *the synthesis of a cycle is at least partially synchronous with and intervenes in the development of the thesis of the next cycle.* For the human beings who operated during the thesis phase of the evolutionary cycle of mankind, the 'seed men' who belonged to the synthesis phase of another related (not necessarily immediately preceding) planetary evolution appear 'divine', but this simply means that they belong to a higher order of being. This higher order is just as 'existential' as that at which human beings operate; it refers to a kind of existence which not only is more encompassing in time and space, but superior in the quality, complexity, and speed of its activities and its responses to cosmic relationship.[1]

This 'superiority' of what religions have called a divine state of power, consciousness, and love-compassion is *relative*. It has

---

[1] What I consider the great misunderstanding embodied in the popularized 'great religions' of the last millennia consists in attributing to whatever is called 'divine' a non-existential character. *Any* 'god' is an existential reality. Even if we speak of the 'One and only God', we refer to *the unity aspect of existence.* 'He' is the one Source of the universe—or at least of *our* universe; but a source is an existential reality, a point of origin, or as Islam states, "the First Point" symbolized by the first letter of the alphabet. *Beyond* this First Point, center of the cosmic Mandala of existence, we have to postulate metaphysical Principles or some symbolical Ocean of Infinite Potentiality from which all existences emerge and to which they withdraw (the alpha and omega of the cosmic cycle). But to speak of such postulated, but forever unknowable and ineffable Mystery as 'God' seems a semantic fallacy. This Mystery is neither being nor non-being. The Hindus referred to It as TAT; the Chinese as TAO. Even the Christian mystic, Meister Eckart, spoke of the Godhead, differentiating it from the 'personal' (because existential) God.

a hierarchical, not an absolute, character; and the term 'hierarchical' here does not refer to a series of graded steps like the rungs of a ladder. If it is used with reference to the system of command in the Army stretching from private to commander-in-chief, it should *only* be in the sense that the mind of a commander-in-chief is supposedly aware of, comprehends, and sustains the *entire* scheme of Army operations, while a private can operate only in his very small and to him usually meaningless field of activity and responsibility. A cosmic hierarchy refers to a series of wholes, each of which *actually contains* all the component lesser forms of existence, while at the same time, it is only a part of a still larger whole.

It is often said that a whole is more than the sum total of its parts; and one thinks of this *plus* factor as being produced by the interactions and interrelatedness of the parts of the whole. But one usually fails to understand that this *plus* factor is also the result of the whole itself being a part of a greater whole whose quality of existence, power, and consciousness pervades the lesser whole, whether or not the latter realizes this to be a fact. When it realizes this fact, it becomes increasingly possible for the greater whole to focus its attention and energy upon the lesser whole constituting one of its component parts. As this occurs, the lesser whole begins to intuitively feel that it has a function to perform within the vaster field of activity that contains it.

This is what I have elsewhere called the principle of *holarchy*. It refers to the 'vertical' relationship between greater and lesser wholes; it is vertical in the sense that the two related wholes operate at different levels of activity. On the other hand, a 'horizontal' relationship exists between wholes which, being at the same level, interact at that level and generate a certain kind of power by such an interaction. The important fact is that the power generated by a horizontal relationship between individual entities operating at the same level of function assumes a special character the moment these entities consciously welcome the fact of their being parts of a greater whole to which they collectively accept a vertical relationship. Then the horizontal relationship acquires a thoroughly functional character and therefore a new meaning. It gains a sacred character the moment the products of the relationship are consciously consecrated to the greater whole.

It is only as this is deeply understood and, if possible, experienced that what today is increasingly glorified as 'group activity' and 'group consciousness' really makes sense. A ritual in which a number of human beings participate is, if adequately performed by dedicated persons, a means of generating a *functional* type of power that polarizes an intervention of the greater whole to which the ritual is consecrated: a vertical relationship is induced—a 'descent' of power from the greater whole to the participants in the ritual. The assumed efficacy of such a process, when it operates adequately, is the basis of all rituals and all theurgical operations.

The modern intellectual mind unfortunately refuses to accept the possibility of such a process. It realizes that when large groups of emotionally aroused people participate in socio-cultural events or activities, impressive results—some of which it calls mass hysteria—can be generated; but these results are attributed to a chain-reaction effect at the horizontal level of interpersonal relationships. Minds conditioned by the empiricism of our science cannot see that in such a collective situation *the power of the culture-whole* also acts through, and in a sense 'possesses', the emotionally aroused participants or spectators whose consciousness is collectively rooted in that culture. This culture-whole is a 'superior' reality—not a figure of speech or an abstract category. It exists at a psychic level. Today we do not have to speak of it as a tribal 'god'; we do not give a 'sacred' character to a political mass-meeting on which the fate of a nation may depend, to a baseball game with thousands of emotionally swayed spectators, or to a vast national mobilization of human energy in time of total war or economic panic. Nevertheless, in such mass situations the culture-whole acts as a collective entity and this action of the 'greater whole'—the nation and its culture—tends to operate through a few persons who, at least in some instances, can be called 'seed men' or at the biological level, 'mutants'.

This discussion may have seemed to take us away from the contrast I established between the 'mythological' and the 'Darwinian' approaches to the problem of building a consistent and significant 'model' of what took place during the first stages of human evolution. Yet since it is so difficult for the modern mind to accept the mythological picture in the personalized and emotional way it has been traditionally formulated, it was necessary for me to try to at least briefly formulate in holistic and holarchic terms the ideas that, I believe, the religious myths meant to convey. The essential point, I repeat, is that when mankind was developing at the strictly biological level (functions of the first order) the powers inherent in the human species, superior beings who represented the spiritual harvest (functions of the fourth order) of another planetary cycle presumably not only 'overshadowed' this earliest phase of human evolution, but actually intervened—directly or indirectly—in that evolution. And this simply refers to the general concept that the end of a cycle acts upon, overshadows or directly intervenes in the early development of a new cycle.

More specifically, because of the essential character of the functions of the fourth order—total inclusiveness and compassion—beings in whom these functions have reached their full development *must* become involved in the evolution of beings who are in the process of actualizing their innate potentialities at the purely biological first level of function. If the consciousness of the latter is aware of the activity of the former, this awareness takes the form of what we usually call 'devotion'. At least in some instances the higher beings may well have taken a physical form or become so intimately involved in the consciousness of a certain lineage of particularly sensitive human beings that they acted as Kings or Teachers. This involvement is not only possible, but natural to beings in whom the functions of the fourth order have reached their full development because, as we saw, the keynote of such an activity is 'interpenetration.'

b. *The Process of Differentiation*

All that has been said so far in this chapter refers to the *thesis* phase of the process of human evolution. The activity of the functions of the first order is the foundation of human evolution; but when human beings reach the level of the individualized and rational mind, the activity of these biological functions either assumes a secondary role devoid of consciously recognized value—they become a routine matter to which little attention is paid—or they may become compulsive in the manner of psychological complexes because they are repressed. Yet the natural process of human evolution brings this automatic and instinctual activity not only to the level of self-consciousness, but to a transmuted and heightened state. When this state is reached, the fully open and illumined mind sees these biological functions as reflections of a higher *cosmic* activity.

In order to consciously apprehend this cosmic activity, directly as well as indirectly in its reflections in the microcosm (the human body), the full development of functions of the fourth order is required. These functions constitute the *synthesis* phase of the dialectical evolutionary process. Between thesis and synthesis stands the *antithesis* which refers to the Age of Differentiation and Conflicts. During that Age, the development of human society passes through four basic stages, each of which provides specific opportunities for the *optimal* development of a conscious and intensified approach to one of the four orders of functional activity.

Differentiation is needed in order to bring the various aspects of human nature and human activity to the state of clear, objective consciousness, and to make possible the emergence of autonomous, self-motivated and responsible individuals from the undifferentiated matrix of the species *homo sapiens*. However, differentiation and individualization imply the development of a sense of separativeness, which leads to pride (or its opposite, shame) and the desire to excel, and almost inevitably at first, to the urge to dominate and rule others. Thus conflicts and war appear. Initially, conflicts between tribal groups simply extend the type of behavior involved in animal and vegetable survival—the need for adequate food and living space. Later on, conflicts between specialized groups within a tribe occur, often fostered by the ambition of men who in some manner have achieved distinction and prestige. Still later, in large cities and within ruling aristocracies, conflicts between individuals hungry for power, wealth and/or sexual conquests become the order of the day.

The stage of 'thesis' in human evolution is one in which human beings are not only active entirely within a natural biospheric environment, but totally pervaded with the rhythms and demands of Earth-nature. Man passively reflects nature and simply seeks to survive and adapt himself as successfully and comfortably as possible to seasonal changes and living conditions. And it seems probable, if not evident, that human beings developed at first in localities where climatic conditions were favorable and the necessities of life were relatively easy to obtain.

The first type of group-organization along strictly biological lines was presumably what has been called the "undivided commune". As the principle of organization was exclusively biological, it most likely took the form of what we define as 'matriarchy' because woman, as mother, was the source of renewed life and thus the great symbol of 'Nature'. Human activity operated exclusively at the level of the first order of functions—thus at the animal level. Yet the seed of the development of higher functions was already *latent* in mankind. Some external factor may have been required to fecundate this seed with the power of the self-conscious and potentially individualized 'mind'; and it is to that factor that I have referred in the preceding pages.

What we are dealing with here is the transition from the functions of the first order to those of the second order—from 'biology' to 'culture'. In the preceding chapter, I associated this transition with the development of sex. But *sexuation* at the strictly biological level—seasonal and totally instinctual sex—is essentially different from *human sexuality*. The fact that in human beings sex is 'a-seasonal' and can be induced at will by what we call imagination—a mental stimulant with immense, even if latent, power—has enormous consequences. So also has the development of an erect spine and especially of formed hands—factors related to the development of human sexuality.[2]

---

[2] In old Hindu books, our present phase of human evolution is described as the period of "hand-power and sex difference" [cf. Bhagavan Das, *The Science of Social Organization* (Adyar, Madras: Theosophical Publishing House, 1910)].

It may indeed be that the reason why according to Genesis 6:2 the Sons of Elohim *married* the daughters of men is that these spiritual-mental beings introduced, not only the centralizing power of 'self-consciousness' into the purely biological mentality of early mankind (the Promethean gift of 'divine fire'), but with it also *the power of imagination.* The power of imagination was what, when connected with the sexual function, transformed animal sex into human sexuality. It also gave to man the ability to think in terms of symbols and, as a result, to transform animal cries and other forms of animal communication into human language and symbolic dance and music. These transformations made possible the development of socio-cultural activity and complex societies.

The impregnation of animal sex with the dynamic and transforming power of the imagination freed human sexuality not only from subservience to seasonal imperatives, but from strictly biological and reproductive purposes. If we believe occult traditions, it led to the magical use of sex and, when degenerated, to 'black magic' and the downfall of 'Atlantis' (whatever was meant by that name). But we do not have to believe such traditions to understand how the non-exclusively biological, imaginative and symbolical development of human sexuality affected the progress—and in some instances, the regression and decadence—of human cultures and societies.

The growth of functions of the second order, the development of agriculture, cattle-raising and, even more, primitive industries requiring the use of fire and metal must have inevitably led from matriarchy to patriarchy. Where superior beings 'married the daughters of men' male dominance may have acquired a special character which presumably led to the formation of a true theocracy. Such a theocracy—if we can take for granted its existence—should be clearly differentiated from much later developments associated with the rule of a *culturally institutionalized* priesthood to which the name of 'theocracy' is also given.

A priesthood is an organization of men who control socio-cultural processes *in the name of* gods or God. The priests, in most cases, do not claim to belong to a 'divine race' distinct from the ordinary human race; they claim the right and duty to perpetuate the teaching of divine beings and to impose upon the culture-whole the commandments and ordinances given by God or His messenger. They preserve what has been released in the more or less distant beginning of a human cycle. A high priest usually claims the ability to communicate mystically or clairaudiently with divine beings and especially to dispense some of their power, but he is not personally a god. However, a true theocracy apparently existed in ancient Egypt because the Pharaoh and his family were definitely considered to belong to a divine race. The same situation was also found in the Inca society in Peru.

In more recent times, we have seen in Japan an imperial dynasty claiming direct descent from creative gods who have been represented in a form suggesting that they belonged to an ancient race of tall beings with much hair and long beards. (The Ainus of the northern islands of Japan may be the last descendants of such a race which probably came from Siberia.) In recent years, however, the members of the imperial family of Japan certainly have lost the characteristics of the supposedly divine race; yet the claim to divinity, accepted by even educated people until Japan's collapse in World War II, remained a powerful factor in Japan's culture. It was nevertheless a 'socio-culturalized' factor revived after the transformation of Japan—a symbol of cultural superiority consciously or semi-consciously meant to balance or counteract the factual power of an encroaching, materialistic Western society.

What was not only accepted as a self-evident *fact* in the *precultural period*—the fabled Golden Age when, according to Greek tradition, gods walked among men—may be retained when the Age of Differentiation and Conflicts begins; but it is retained and used as a powerful symbol of integration. A society developing strictly at the level of functions of the first order operates in terms of what, to its members, are 'facts'. When these facts lose their character of self-evident, or unquestionably perceptible, reality—when they become memories to which a deep symbolical meaning is attached—the stage of 'thesis' is passed. Tribal unanimity of itself, no longer factually exists; it has to be perpetuated in some manner by a type of men acting as preservers of a glorified past. What was an inner, psychically compulsive, and quasi-instinctual reality becomes increasingly more conscious—and later on, resented—subservience of differentiated personalities to a code of laws and a divinely sanctioned tradition.

A somewhat analogous situation exists in the traditional family and the relationship between children and parents. The new-born child is psychically one with the mother. The infant's organism still vibrates in a kind of unison with his progenitors; he is still psychically enveloped, especially when breast-fed, by the mother's electro-magnetic field—a psychic womb. One may speak of the utter devotion of the baby to his mother and call it 'love', but it is not love in a strictly human and conscious sense because it is the compelling manifestation of a biopsychic fact. Sooner or later, the psychic umbilical cord becomes thin, or it may suddenly break. Yet the combination of strong memory-patterns, habit and a deep sense of insecurity—plus the pressure of parental authority and fear of punishment—usually forces the relationship of the child and his parents to retain for some time what may superficially appear to be the same kind of devotional aspect

The character of this relationship nevertheless has changed; from *biopsychically factual* and unquestionable, it has become *socio-cultural* and open to question. It is increasingly being molded by religion and cultural tradition—a particular way of life. As this happens, the probability—and always to some extent, the inevitability—of conflicts begins to manifest. The process of differentiation has started. It takes the form of the growth of the *ego-function;* and after the mental faculties and the discursive, argumentative intellect develop, individualization gradually takes place.

Then the exercise of social and physical control *has to* begin in order to manage the centrifugal and potentially explosive development of a myriad of ego-wills. The necessary control is exercised by men of physical power and intense will—that is by a 'warrior caste'. When, later on, mental forces begin to increasingly operate in the people upon whom patterns of *physical* order and group security have been imposed by the 'strong men' of a turbulent and formative period, another class of human beings is called upon to build *mental* patterns of order and security. These are needed to keep increasingly eager, questioning—and thus potentially doubting—minds within a *socio-culturally safe* realm of enquiry and investigation. This new class of human beings *uses* the collective memory-remains of the precultural Age (the 'thesis' phase of human evolution) to build a system of intellectual control. This system depends upon clearly formulated dogmas (or paradigms), emotionally inspiring symbols and myths, and the periodic experience of participation in rituals—both religious and, later on, socio-cultural—during which the root-unity of the community becomes *an evident fact of consciousness.*

The combination of these factors at the intellectual, emotional, and physical levels of human activity keep the development of a culture-whole within a particular area referring to only one of the many potentialities inherent in the human species. The men who perform this function form a priesthood; and institutions of philosophical and scientific learning are built whose essential purpose is to define, strengthen, and deepen—but also inevitably to limit—the special character of the society and its culture.

After a while, when this work has been performed, other forces come into play within the social organism. A new type of activity gradually attains prominence. Its nature and purpose is to expand the field of the culture-whole by the medium of 'commerce'—that is, through the interplay and eventually the merging of various types of human beings and diverse culture-wholes. A 'merchant class' rises to power. It contains within its activities the germ of its downfall—as every class actually does. This leads to the last phase of the Age of Differentiation and Conflicts.

The nature of this phase is complex and little understood, because it marks the possibility of a basic change of level—either in terms of biological, cultural, and spiritual disintegration, or, a radical transformation of human existence. Such a transformation is possible only to individuals and groups of individuals who learn to operate—even if only hesitantly and at first confusedly—at the level of functions of the fourth order.

I shall now briefly outline some of the most characteristic

manifestations of the four phases through which a culturally organized social collectivity of human beings passes during the Age in which opportunities are provided to develop differentiated capacities and skill, but also during which conflicts inevitably arise when a dynamic and transformative minority comes to embody the adequate answer to a new evolutionary need and succeeds in controlling the social mechanisms of power and productivity.

5

THE PATTERN OF DIFFERENTIATION AND CONFLICT

According to the dialectical model of evolution outlined in the preceding chapters, a cycle of existence begins in a state of unity and witnesses a process of differentiation resulting in a multiplicity of existential forms and lines of development, all of which eventually converge. In the end these constitute a complex 'multi-une' whole in which what in the beginning was only a potentiality is finally found perfectly actualized.

So stated, however, the model fails to convey what we can assume to be a universal fact, if properly understood in its varied manifestations. This fact is that, at least in the universe we experience, all existence operates on a dualistic basis. Whenever a new kind of energy—a new source of useable power—is released and made available, its use can lead human beings to advance a step further toward the end-fulfillment of the purpose inherent in the entire existential cycle; but on the other hand, the misuse of that power—or the failure to use it because of fear—starts a process of disintegration.

When I presented a picture of the first period of human evolution—the 'thesis'—I stated that, unless we accepted the limiting materialistic bias of our empirical scientific mentality, we had earnestly to try to understand what is implied in the practically universal tradition according to which, during that first period (or at least part of it), quasi-divine beings lived on this Earth together with a nascent and still semi-animal mankind. These beings brought to men, not only some knowledge of how to deal with the seed-multiplying process of life (agriculture and cattle raising), but also the 'seed' of self-consciousness and the promise of autonomous and self-reliant individuality. Thus a dualistic situation prevailed. As we reach the period of 'anti-thesis'—of differentiation of human types and social conflicts—we also find that during every phase of the collective evolution of *society*, the development of a new type of socio-psychological function also operates at two levels.

There must be differentiation in order to provide means of expression and perfection to all the basic aspects implied in the original theme of 'Man'. Man as an archetype is a 'cosmos'—a complex system of potentialities of manifestation, or we might say, a highly condensed set of solutions to an immense variety of existential possibilities and problems of relationship. All these potentialities have to be developed as socio-psychological characteristics—as differentiated faculties to be consciously and deliberately used in a variety of collective (interpersonal and inter-group) situations. These situations may produce an ever greater variety of constructive or destructive results.

Traditionally the pattern of development of a culture-whole during the Age of Differentiation has a fourfold character. (Karl Marx in his materialistic approach to history merely reformulated traditional concepts in a new way required by the new situation created by the Industrial Revolution.) This fourfold character pervades the world in which man operates at this stage of evolution, called by American Indians the Fourth World and to which the Hebrew refers when speaking of the Tetragrammaton. We are living in a state of nature in which four elements or conditions of substance are in evidence—the fourth one not yet readily perceptible or understood: solid (earth), liquid (water), gaseous (air) and plasma (the 'fire' of ancient philosophers and alchemists). Man can develop at four levels of functional activity—the fourth one today being equally difficult for most people to comprehend. Similarly, in the development of a culture-whole, four periods can be detected, at least theoretically, once we cease being hypnotized by the detail of outer events and pay attention to the slowly shifting focus of socio-psychological growth.

The first period is primarily of physical activity concerned with the possession of land and of the means of productivity. These include human beings (who are attached to the land), as well as animals. They refer to biological factors and to the development of a new genetic type through marriage, rape, or slavery.

The second period is primarily occupied with the preservation, consolidation, cultivation, and refinement of values acquired during the preceding period—thus with the development of institutions which serve as molds for a specific way of collective behavior, feeling and thinking. Socio-political laws, religious dogmas, and philosophic-scientific paradigms are developed, enforced by collective instrumentalities. These essentially are a police force—a clergy wielding the dreaded power of excommunication, and in some instances, of physical imprisonment or death —committees of scholars and 'academies', not only defining specific modes of thinking and formulation, but curtailing those that are unacceptable to an institutionalized mentality and effectively ostracizing the people promoting them.

The third period witnesses the growth of trade, the spread of interpersonal and intercultural relationships, and as a result, the expansion of production. Intellectual faculties are stimulated because the analytical, managerial, engineering power of the discursive minds is required to deal successfully with the consequence of all forms of expansion. In order to cope with the new social situations and the tensions they produce at the family level as well as in progressively larger cities, men, then women, and later on even children are impelled to develop strong egos. At first selfishness, greed for the anonymous social power of wealth, and the demand for ever-increasing social productivity to meet the wants of always more demanding 'consumers' are contained within the restraining patterns of activity built during the second period; but these patterns gradually stretch to a point at which they lose their resilience. They finally break down once the centralizing and integrating symbols and values that ensouled them lose, first, their 'sacred' character, then their credibility.

As the forms through which these values were expressed become vulgarized, and intellectual, emotional, sexual, and social restraints are no longer observed—mainly because the class of human beings whose function it was to convincingly embody them has succumbed to the pressures of socio-economic changes

—a fourth period begins. On the one hand, it leads to a more or less critical state of chaos; on the other hand, it polarizes the appearance of at least a few Promethean men—men whose inspired and transformative minds often dwell in intense, but often tragic personalities still deeply affected by the chaotic vibrations and the traumatic or unrelenting pressures of their deteriorating civilization. Some of these transformative-creative men—and now also women—release *mind-seeds* that in due time fecundate the inchoate masses—the human substance of a future culture-whole.

In what follows, I shall briefly discuss some of the most characteristic features of the four types of human beings; but at first, in order to avoid confusion, I should make it clear that I am no longer dealing with the *planetary* evolution of mankind as a whole, but with the development of *local* societies. Some of these societies follow one another in time and are related mainly through a spiritual kind of inheritance; others develop synchronously in different regions of the Earth and their interactions at a certain time of their life-cycle lead to more or less far-reaching transformations.

In the first instance, the principle already mentioned as an explanation for the mythological belief that quasi-divine beings taught primitive mankind agriculture and the arts of civilization applies also, but at a different level. The last phase of a parent-culture is synchronous with the progressively destructive, or at least radically transforming, impact of more primitive races or tribes. In the end, these tribes replace the old disintegrating society, inheriting from it the land, what remains of the people, and a harvest of social and spiritually transforming new values. The social achievements and at times the intoxicated visions of 'seed men' produced by the old culture provide the mixture of people from the old society and the conquering tribes with a basic set of great symbols and fecundating ideas. The slowly developing new culture-whole that inherited these images and concepts embodies them in institutions which nevertheless are stamped with the characteristic temperament of the conquerors.

How this process operates is clearly shown when one studies the rise and migrations of Germanic tribes at the time the Roman Empire (the last phase of a Mediterranean Greco-Latin culture-whole) was gradually losing its vitality and disintegrating. It is also shown in the final breakdown of the empire under the onslaught of the 'barbarians' and finally, in the centuries of the so-called Dark Ages when the European society was being formed through unceasing conflicts. During these conflicts, a Warrior Type dominated the European stage; but other forces were also active which after a while led to the development of a new type—each new type 'gestating', as it were, during the period of ascendancy of the preceding one.

a. *The Warrior and the Ruler*

Whether we consider what seemingly occurred in ancient India when Aryan races swept down into what now is Pakistan, in Mexico when successive invasions by northern tribes conquered the more southern plateaus or the still lower regions where the Mayan culture once flourished, in China when Mogols and later Manchu 'barbarians' subjugated the coastal lands, or in Europe when Germanic tribes invaded the corrupt and tottering Roman Empire that controlled the entire Mediterranean region, we witness a basically similar pattern of development. A dynamic group of tribes, which very often (though perhaps not always) had been set in motion by climatic changes or the need for food for an expanding population, 'descend' from relatively northern regions upon the land occupied by a once flourishing but now effete and slowly disintegrating society.

The outcome of this encounter varies according to the character and the relative strength of the contending forces. In some cases, it would seem that the rough invaders are more readily absorbed into the old culture, which is thus revitalized and transformed, yet retains its fundamental character. This may occur when the conquered *land* has very powerful characteristics which compel the conquerors to accept basic ways of life and modes of thinking required for the survival of *any* society regardless of its particular culture and institutions. In other cases, the old culture is radically transformed, yet the basic values and symbols which structure the development of the new society, after the invaders have destroyed most of the *outer* institutionalized forms of the old culture, are nevertheless values and symbols that had originated within the last phase of the old society—its harvest of social and spiritual seeds.

In the well-known case of the transformation of the Greco-Latin Mediterranean into the Medieval European culture, the essential ideas-symbols inherited from the old by the new society can be condensed into two powerful worlds: Caesar and Christ. It is around these two archetypes that the European culture has evolved and become polarized. The first one refers to what I have called the Administrative Order; the other, to the Creative Order. However, during the first period of the European cycle, the Germanic chieftain was the dominant figure. He might lead a relatively large group of tribes or only a small band of restless people in search of land for survival. But in all cases wherever we can speak of the Warrior Type, we see it operating as a dynamic, muscular and willful power.

It acts at first as destroyer of a sclerotic and spiritually empty society which it had infiltrated through the device of mercenary service. Symbolically speaking, the Warrior chews and breaks down the forms of the past, releasing the human contents of these socio-cultural forms as 'chemicals' which will form a part of the humus of the future society. Cities are turned into ruins; aqueducts are destroyed or left inoperative; in many places the cultivation of the soil becomes nearly impossible; roadbeds break down; life becomes localized and disuniversalized. The land is divided into relatively small domains into which insecure men, women and children are herded under the protection of the Warriors' muscular power, and later of massive fortifications. In some instances, vestiges of the dying Roman culture briefly survive when Germanic chieftains try to imitate the mode of life of provincial Roman administrators.

This image of the powerful administrator, only distantly related to a central source of authority, begins to blend with the more primitive biological-tribal image of the chieftain as a powerful male supreme in war, and gradually a Ruler Type is formed. To such a type, the old imperial ideal of Caesar appears as a goal to strive after—and in Medieval European society, we see the prototypal personality of Charlemagne claiming a Caesarian type of position and being glorified and made into a myth by Medieval bards.

In other countries and societies, powerful leaders, as they come to such a position of power over disparate racial elements, claim the attribute of divinity—the Persian kings of the sixth century B. C. being perhaps the model that the Roman Caesars sought to imitate.[1] This claim should be considered a conscious or subconscious attempt to revive the archetypal image of divine king-hierophants. In our European culture-whole, a time came when the 'divine right' of kings was widely accepted, but the power of the Christian Church made it impossible for the kings to claim an actual state of divinity.

Whatever claim is being made to justify and sanction the position of ruler, and especially of absolute ruler, the psycho-social fact is that men of the Warrior class or caste (in India, the *Kshattriyas*), under the pressure of circumstance and in order to meet the developing need for centralization of command, emerge as exemplars of a higher form of the Warrior Type, the Ruler Type. What differentiates the latter from the former is the Ruler's ability to organize or administer the field of effective power that he has built or has inherited, often through murder or ruthless conquest. The Warrior Type has no characteristic ability for organization. His power is biological and strictly personal. He conquers; he does not really 'rule'. To rule is to measure, to establish stable patterns of relationship centered around a source of power which, though at first still personal, nevertheless implies some sort of innate destiny or vocation.

It was fashionable to speak of the English, and before them

---

[1] The Persian model of an all-powerful quasi-divine king may be derived from the Indian ideal of the Universal Monarch or *Cakravartin* "pacifying mankind by incorporating under his sole sovereignty all the kingdoms." He was considered "equal in rank to those of the world-redeeming Buddhas . . . [They both] manifest the same universal principle" on the secular and the spiritual plane respectively. This concept was reflected during the European Middle Ages in the dualism of Pope and Emperor—a most distorted reflection manifesting as a long and bitter struggle for supremacy. Cf. Heinrich Zimmer, *Philosophies of India,* "The Universal King", p. 129ff.

the old Romans, as a 'race of rulers'. The capacity to effectively rule demands an innate ability to *manipulate* people and to create favorable conditions for the growth of power. It therefore transcends the purely biological-physical level of activity, inasmuch as it requires for its successful operation a conscious or instinctive 'resonance' to the integrative power of the life-force; and at the physical level that power operates as the capacity to act as a focal point for the centralization of the varied activities of several organs, each representing a particular function.

This need for centralization compels any effective ruler to operate through a hierarchical chain of command—which means, in the most general sense of the term, a 'bureaucracy'. The Persian king, Darius, may have been the first outstanding example of a founder of an efficient bureaucracy of administrators (satraps), though he may have been influenced by previous Egyptian and Indian models. Perhaps more than any other absolute monarch of the Age of Differentiation and Conflicts, he represents the Ruler type in its most characteristic aspect—a ruler who by claiming to be 'divine, imitated' the prehistoric kings-hierophants of more-than-human origin. His support of the traditional founder of the Zoroastrian religion could be said to exemplify the dual manifestation of supreme socio-cultural power —the coupling of King and High Priest. In Europe this dualism of power took the form of Emperor and Pope. While the Pope theoretically embodied the Christ-Image and (through 'Apostolic Succession') the spiritual, transformative and redeeming power of the Son of God, the Emperor fulfilled the archetypal Caesarian role of ruler and integrator of an extensive culture-whole.

The appearance of the Ruler Type on a social stage indicates not only the collective need for administrative power-centralization, but the soon-apparent necessity of giving a superphysical religious *sanction* to absolute power. In the prehistoric period, if truly superhuman and at least quasi-divine beings were *actually* present and utterly dominated the human situation, this domination would have been, I repeat, *a self-evident fact*, so great was the difference of level of consciousness and potential activity between them and still very primitive human beings; but at the time of Darius, the claim for divinity could not be

supported by factual evidence—the mere ability to conquer and
build an empire being essentially different from the fact of
belonging to a superior race. Thus the claim had to be 'sanctioned', i.e., made *sacred*. It had to be referred back to a creative
moment of origin, thus to the ritualistic and symbolic life of a
Prophet or Avatar. In the European culture-whole, this meant
Christ. The ruler thus assumed the function of "Defender of the
Faith." He had to be 'sacralized' by the Representative of Christ
in this world, the Pope. This led to the complex ritual of a
king's coronation by the Pope, or at least by the bishops in
whom the power of the Apostolic Succession is said to dwell since
their sacramental ordination.

b. *The Priest and the Philosopher*

The social function of what I call here the Priest Type, whatever name its representatives have in their particular religion, is
to maintain the integrity and the tradition of a culture. It is *not*
a spiritual function, in the sense in which I use the term, spiritual, i.e., as referring to a creative, originating activity.[2] It may
be a proselytizing function if the religion of the culture has an
expansionistic character, especially during the growth of the
society; but essentially, the Priest Type is that of 'the Preserver'
—the second aspect of the Hindu Trinity, Vishnu. It is true that
in any religion the priest deals with individual persons and ca-
ters to their supposedly spiritual needs; but what is actually
meant by such needs is the ability to function adequately and
wholly *within* the particular culture in which these persons are
born, and therefore to use their biological and psychic energies
in a 'cultured' instead of a 'wild' manner—or, more crudely
stated, in a *human* rather than an animal and instinctual way.

The functions of both the Ruler and the Priest Types is to
stand as impressive and efficacious symbols of the development
of functions of the second order; thus, of the triumph of culture
over biology. Both are charged with the responsibility of making

---

[2] Cf. my book, *Culture, Crisis and Creativity* (Wheaton: Theosophical
Publishing House, 1976).

sure that biological-instinctual drives are at least *contained* within, and whenever possible *transformed* by various types of socio-cultural devices—on the one hand by laws, regulations and physical punishments, and on the other hand, by sacraments and a pervasive kind of morality having been formulated or at least implied in an original Revelation. This Revelation is derived from the quality of the life, the actual deeds and the pronouncements of the Avatar or Prophet, and of the great 'seed men' who lived and died *just before* the cycle of the new culture-whole began—thus during the last period of a preceding culture-whole.

These facts should be fairly obvious when we consider a particular culture-whole born in a specific locality and developing within a more or less definite region—which may or may not be the place of origin. If transposed to the larger field of the planetary evolution of the whole of humanity, the extension of these facts should provide with us a rationale for the traditional belief in the existence of superior beings from a previous evolutionary life-scheme who gave to nascent mankind an 'Original Revelation' from which what has been variously called 'the universal Wisdom-Religion' 'the great Tradition' or 'the perennial philosophy' had initially been derived. What does not seem clear to many people using these terms is that they refer to the *planetary evolution* of mankind as a whole all over the globe, and not to any *particular and localized* culture-whole (or in Toynbee's sense, Society or Civilization). These two levels of development should not be confused, even if any fully developing culture-whole tends to develop along lines similar to those operative within the much larger field of the global evolution of mankind.

By virtue of its function, the Priest Type is conservative. It is a 'religious' function, because it literally 'binds back' (*religere*) the developing functions of the second order to a creative Source, a transformative descent of the Holy Spirit which, I repeat, antedates the concrete beginnings of the culture the priest serves. A religion opens a particular path for the transformation and rebirth of persons born within a particular culture; however, if a person succeeds, primarily by his or her own strength and determination, to reach the consummating and also consuming end of that path, he or she becomes suspicious to the priesthood. The mystic is not welcome in institutionalized religions, especially if a more or less hereditary or class-conscious priesthood has become involved in the politics of social power. If tolerated and glorified after the mystic's death, the mystical experience has to be formulated in terms of religious orthodoxy in order to be fitted into the socio-cultural scheme.

Generally speaking, the development of functions of the fourth order, in whatever way they operate in the unusual person, has to be translated into terms of functions of the second order in order to be acceptable to the religious institutions. Similarly, any new and superior way of releasing physically operative power is at first blocked by existing social-economic institutions profiting from or used to the old method until they can absorb and control the production and effective use of the new type of energy. In most instances, the reluctant acceptance and implied change occur only after a social crisis made the need for new sources of power imperative. Sometimes, the religious priesthood *seems* to welcome the individual who, through the traditional methods has achieved what these methods were meant to produce when originally outlined. When this occurs, however, the question is whether the achievement *really* has a universalistic, all-inclusive character. As seen from the point of view of fully developed fourth order functions, it may have only a *relatively* universalistic character—just like the statement by intellectuals in ancient Rome that nothing human could be alien to them had actual validity only within the range of an enlarged, yet limited, Mediterranean world.

The important point here is whether the universalism of functions of the fourth order can ever be reached without a full development of the localized and limiting functions of the second order; and in all but at least relatively exceptional cases, the answer seems to be that without a firm socio-cultural foundation, the fourth level of functional activity cannot be actually *reached*, even though there appears to be a direct connection between the biological and the spiritual. Even if there is such a connection, what is implied is that the biological level may *reflect* the spiritual. A reflection, however, is not an active creative reality. In order to reach the creative reality of the fourth level of functional activity, a human being should not only have developed socio-cultural values, but also have become 'individualized' through the operation of functions of the third order. Such an operation begins at the collective level of cultural and social processes with the development of a Philosopher type.

In socio-cultural terms, the Philosopher type is also that of the Scholar. The Philosopher is the person who either belongs to a 'school of philosophy' or starts (or allows to form) such a school. As it grows in influence, the school tends to become institutionalized into what in the Western world we call a college or university. Literally speaking, a 'college' deals with a whole system of 'laws'; and by law, what is actually meant is a method allowing us to comprehend and use for our own individual or collective purpose the *order* we believe to be inherent in nature and the universe.

While the Ruler and his priesthood simply seek to preserve and enforce the outer forms of the collective life-ordering derived from a previous creative Revelation, the Philosopher seeks to understand and to adequately formulate either what he feels to be behind the Revelation, or the order he perceives or intuitively realizes to exist in the universe. The Philosopher's endeavors imply the development of a more or less objective mind. At first he may be mainly an 'apologist' for the official religion of his culture; but eventually, the drive toward objectivity in understanding leads to the development of intellectual process of comparative and psychological analysis, and the critical faculty develops. Sooner or later, criticism unavoidably implies crisis; that is, a 'decision'—a 'cutting away' from a taken-for-granted acceptance of intellectual paradigms, religious dogmas and moral imperatives which represent at the socio-cultural level what biological instincts and taboos had once been at the totally compulsive level of biology and tribal organization.

A particular type of Philosopher arises whose function it is to initiate a process of socio-cultural transformation at the level of ideas. In one culture, he is Socrates forcing the intellectuals of his day to question everything. In another, he is Nietzsche announcing the "twilight of idols" and "the death of God"—the

God of our Christian-European culture with its roots in a but partially understood ancient Greek culture. To this type belong the men who start, and often over-indulge in the 'higher criticism' of religious records—and psychologists like Freud and his school of 'reductionists' trying to prove that the assumed greatness of revered products of their slowly dying culture 'merely is', or is 'nothing but', a more or less aberrant manifestation of some biopsychological functions.

After these crisis-inducing philosophers-muckrakers have done their necessary—even if catabolic—work, another aspect of the Philosopher Type enters the stage of the by then highly disturbed, if not conflict-racked society. These philosophers try tentatively to integrate the original themes of the culture and the new values promoted by the crisis-philosophers. They are the first 'seed men' of the culture-whole, and though their culture may stay alive for a long time after their deaths, some of their realizations may be transferred (as 'seed ideas') to the future culture-whole, at least in a radically modified form. Plato and Aristotle belong to that type—Plato trying to combine the power of the Orphic-Pythagorean tradition and the challenging character of the discursive intellect (the function of transition leading from the second to the third order) whose development Socrates pioneered; Aristotle emphasizing the implication of the new function and its *potential* universalistic character—thus paving the way to the future emergence of the Scientist type.

At first, the Scientist is still very close to the Philosopher in his endeavor to provide an intellectualized and rationalized model of the universe; but as Baconian empiricism supersedes the intuitive and metaphysical rationalism of the Greek philosophers, and an experimental methodology excludes from the field of scientific validity all that transcends or diverges from the sense-data and mathematical "rigorous thinking" (Bertrand Russell), the Scientist gives up any form of reliance upon what he calls philosophical speculation. Yet in time, as we shall see, the very achievements of science and its progeny, technology, produce situations which irresistibly impel the greatest scientists to ask not only philosophical, but metaphysical questions; a 'philosophy of science' seeks to answer these questions.

In order to understand what Western science has brought to mankind, we have to integrate its function within a larger process dealing with the expansion of interpersonal and intercultural relationships. This expansion is spearheaded by the appearance of new types of human beings in which a new aspect of archetypal Man seeks its full and differentiated development. The French word *commercant,* unfortunately missing from the English language, expresses most precisely the basic function of this type. Through persons of this type, a 'commergence' of human activities and individual or group interest takes place through 'commerce'—which means through interchange and trading. The term, business, refers only to the externality of the process—i.e., the fact that it keeps people 'very busy' indeed. They are busy exchanging goods and services; but one can only exchange what one possesses.

Commerce and the expansion of human activity it engenders require products to exchange and trade with. As a result, what could be called the Producer Type acquires a specialized importance. Productivity takes on a character and a meaning which basically differs from what it was in the archaic Ages. It becomes industrialized, and this gives it a seemingly unbounded and almost infinitely expansive character which has very basic repercussions on the wholesome development of the human person. *Commerce* and *productivity* act as powerful agents in the wholesale process of individualization; and we saw already that this process essentially characterizes the Age of Differentiation and Conflict (antithesis).

c. *The Trader and the Producer*

Two basically different types of trading and production have to be considered, even if the second type gradually develops from the first. In the early stages of agriculture, production operates at the strictly biological level as a means to survival, and there is usually no surplus. If there is, it is probably preserved to alleviate the distress caused by a year of drought or by flooding and other calamities. Production is strictly local, and it affects the operation of the biological functions. When trading begins, it takes the form of barter which, most likely at first, does not involve the development of any new functions— only a kind of 'cunning' which constitutes the first stage of the development of a type of human intelligence hardly superior to animal instinct.

Some of the first products to be traded are probably salt, perhaps some spices, and objects of ornamentation for women. When trade involves the exchange of commodities whose rarity and attractiveness tend to make them standards of value, trade acquires a socio-cultural character, and we can speak of it literally as 'commerce' because it brings together groups of people of at least somewhat different cultures or cultural status; it incites different types of human beings to 'co-merge' in certain localities and at definite times of the year. The *market place* begins to take on an intercultural character. The products of one group or village are compared with those of another. Competition and specialization develop. Eventually a Merchant class arises which displays some characteristic mental and emotional features. These lead to the growth of possessiveness and greed for wealth —wealth now being increasingly represented by not only *the marketable value* of what is produced, but *the ability to sell products at a profit;* and profit more and more takes the form of accumulatable money.

Money is at the socio-cultural level what, to some extent, hormones are at the biological level. Hormones control the growth and the balance of functional activity in the biological organism. As money circulates in an organized society, it carries with it social power—that is, it makes possible or enhances productivity, whether it be physical-biological or artistic-cultural productivity. When concentrated in a particular class of people, or in the hands of a powerful individual or family, it can incite and support another group of persons who, in return for money, *specialize* in producing a particular kind of wares or service. When specialized, production acquires a new character. It becomes *technologized*. This requires the development of the technical mind which specializes in the invention of new means of production. The nature of these means of production differs according to the state of intellectual development of the Philosopher and Scientist type; but whether these means are slaves or machines requiring a 'proletariat' to operate them, the new type of productivity-for-profit gives rise to a *bourgeoisie*.

In Europe, this class—the *Tiers Etat* (Third Estate) rising after a period of protracted conflict between the Emperor and the Pope—is at first a class of merchants, but the Trader Type assumes an ever more dominant role. The men of this type are personally eager to increase their wealth, social power and prestige, while at the same time, they are more or less unconsciously compelled by the need inherent in the culture-whole to expand the intensity of its *internal* dynamism (by linking more closely provinces and towns) and the scope of its *outreaching* activity (by interacting with external culture-wholes). By calling for a more abundant and specialized productivity, the mercantile class stimulates the inventiveness of an elite group of engineers whose technological inventions achieve the transformation of the old, strictly biologically conditioned—even if religiously inclined—peasantry living close to the soil and attuned to seasonal rhythms. Sooner or later, the bourgeoisie absorbs every other social class through the lure of profit and the bait of money-power.

This dynamic development and actual (even if camouflaged) triumph of the bourgeoisie has varied consequences. It changes the internal patterns of society's operations; it also has a radically transformative effect upon the psychological functioning of the members of the society. As the society expands through increasing relationships with other culture-wholes—relationships which in many cases manifest as the ruthless conquest of more primitive races still operating at a strictly biological-cultural level—the defining patterns of the society's collective organizations and the religious and educational sanctions that gave them psychic and intellectual solidity gradually lose their cohesion and credibility. They slowly but irremediably break down; and the change in the psychological character of the members of the society—already brought about by the accelerated development of the discursive, analytical mind and the incitements of the profit motive—assumes a radical character. Human beings under

mounting psychological and social pressures find themselves uprooted by the tidal process of individualization. They react by
developing increasingly abrasive and alienated egos.

In a very real sense, the ego can be related to the Trader Type.
It uses relationship for profit; and profit means an increase in
size or a strengthening and decoration of what constitutes the
circumference of the personal being. What is usually called the
self is the *center* of the being; the ego is essentially the power
that deals with the security, health and comfort of that part of
the total being which, because as a circumference it is in constant
contact with the outside world, is affected by, and also strives to
affect, whatever surrounds the personality; and circumference
may mean the actual borders of a nation, or the psychic as well
as physical boundaries of the organized field of activity we call
an individual person.

Initially, as a feudal domain or nation attempts to establish a
safe frontier or expand its borders until its conquest of the environment is definitely checked, it is the Warrior Class (usually
assisted by the priests) that is in charge of the operations. The
process of growth has a quasi-biological character which demands strength, daring and the kind of almost animal cunning
we call, at least in its early stages, diplomacy. But as a Merchant Class assumes power, another kind of expansion develops,
eventually taking precedence over the physico-biological kind in
which the Warrior Type excelled: mercantile and economic expansion. As this occurs, the Warrior Class not only takes a relatively secondary role, it backs with physical force the mercantile
adventures which have become the dominant (even if perhaps
not officially mentioned) social function—but it changes its character and becomes what is called 'the Military' or 'the Services';
later on, it is further transformed into an army of mercenaries.

Mercantile and economic expansion result from the growth
of the bourgeoisie, and it also feeds such a growth. The great difference between a warrior-type of expansion and trade expansion is that in the first case, expansion means either the killing
or physical enslavement of human beings and often the destruc-
tion of the resources of the land, while in the case of trading,

the people to which one sells goods, and even the land from which one extracts materials needed for industrial production, must be kept in a condition of relative well-being, otherwise the 'colonized' people could not buy manufactured wares or provide conqueror's factories with necessary raw materials. Thus the relationship between the conqueror and the conquered—who may be allowed to retain the appearance of freedom—takes on a special character; it is 'relationship for profit'.

What applies to a nation intent upon mercantile and economic expansion ('economic' referring here to the 'loaning' (!) of money to serve as capital to feed the trade operations) applies also to the individual person in the process of developing an ego. The ego *uses* relationship to other people in order to satisfy the desires of the personal being—desires for comfort, pleasure, social prestige, and also what is called 'love'. These desires (or wants) refer to the circumference of being, because they can only be satisfied by some form of exchange with other beings in the more or less immediate surroundings. They do not primarily refer to basic biological *needs;* the satisfaction of these needs is instinctively sought by the organism itself, by muscular activity, by hunting and quasi-animal cunning. What the ego characteristically *wants*, it seeks through the clever manipulation of its relationships with other egos; and this often implies the use of deceit —the ego-form of decoy and camouflage.

A bourgeois society thus becomes a society of egos, ruled by egos especially adept at dealing with social processes and getting around various kinds of laws and regulations, and for the glorification of the one essential goal of ego-activity, *success.* Such a society is adequately characterized and symbolized by the 'American dream' of ever-increasing individual wealth and power, backed by a typical quasi-religious 'New Thought' glorifying health, wealth and happiness—and business. The keyword of this mercantile society is *productivity.* The Gross National Product must always rise; there must be more of everything, not only at the physical level, but at the emotional and mental levels as well. Trade operates not only in terms of exchange of products, raw and industrially manufactured, but also through the interpenetration of cultures and ideas. This leads to a Babel of tongues, a melting pot of concepts, symbols and vestigial traditions.

Every person, regardless of social conditioning, race, color and religion must be considered equal; but 'equal' in what sense, and at what level? Such a question is not asked because, when the ego is lord, "every man is a king"; but if every man is a king, kingship as an office no longer has any meaning. In fact, when this happens, no *function* has any humanly essential and inspiring meaning. Meaning has come to reside only in the fact of being 'an individual' functionally unrelated to anything else and *therefore* an abstract entity—a citizen considered merely as a voting unit, a number within a statistical percentage. Percentage has become the ruling principle of the society.

Theoretically, this could mean that the 'greater number'—thus the masses—rule. But this is the supreme social illusion; the masses never rule. During the later period of the culture-whole, they are ruled by the promoters of fashions—whether in clothing, in thinking or in the arts—who themselves are merely puppets or mediums controlled by Karma—that is, by the accumulating pressure of cultural sclerosis or senescence and the tragic fate of having to constantly produce new thrills, new gadgets and new techniques. For an ego-rewarding moment, the attention of the masses can only fix upon something that will allow a few persons to act as 'the beautiful people'—or as the leader, the star, the psychologist or the swami in the spotlight—and the rest, to imitate them.

An unconscious type of servility can hide under the cloak of individual freedom. Even if sheer, inorganic power inheres in the aroused masses, its fate-ordained display reveals the essential impotence of power detached from function. When a society reaches the last phase of its organic existence, it tends to be seized by spasms of dysfunction because neither the group of individuals who actually control social productivity, wealth and police power, nor the 'proletariat'—whether in suburban bourgeois attire or in festering tenements—can any longer feel, think and act in functional relationship to the culture-whole.

Yet even the illusion of freedom can be turned into the reality of severance; and mass-servility to fashion and ephemeral dictators can act as a polarizing force to spur the rise of 'seed' men and women who, after breaking away from the binding power of relationships that have become a 'dance of death', self-consecrate their lives and total being to the service of a new descent of creative power.

d. *The Money-Conditioned Types and the Transpersonal Individual*

Wherever the bourgeoisie becomes the dominant factor in a society, the drive toward ever-increasing productivity, personal success and socio-political power takes the near-singular form of the acquisition and secure possession of *money*. While we can single out and characterize various types of human beings occupying the various rungs of the social ladder, they nevertheless all have a common feature; they all want money and live primarily in terms of the acquisition of money or the preservation and increase of possessions which in the last analysis can almost always be resolved into sums of money. Money conditions every aspect of the personal as well as social life, and in the majority of cases, it not only conditions, but actually determines the character and development of human beings, giving them common features—even though these human beings are proudly insisting on their individual freedom of opinion, choice and behavior.

At one end of the social ladder, we find the wealthy capitalist, the prodigiously successful executive and speculator, the billionaire; at the other end, we see proletarians belonging to some minority group living in squalid tenements or broken down cottages on non-productive land. But the lives and minds of both the very rich and the very poor are equally haunted by money. The profit-motive dominates the collective mentality of everyone as surely and inescapably as a political totalitarian regime dominates the lives of its people. In fact, the power of money is more tyrannical in our supposedly most democratic and 'free' American society than in harshly repressive Communist countries where certain basic material needs are at least supplied without charge to everyone. From this we might deduce that human beings, collectively considered, can hardly avoid being at least partially the slaves of a dominant social power. When it is not a theocratic church, an absolute monarch or a Communist Politbureau, these external tyrannies are replaced by that of money. The whip of the profit-system can lash the soul and mind of human beings as thoroughly as that of the slave-master; the only difference is that in the first instance, men are left the illusion of freedom. In natural jungles, animals are dominated by hunger; in urban jungles people may also crave money only for food, but because of development of infinitely complex socio-cultural patterns and individualized ambition, in a vast number of human lives the passion for money spreads over the whole psyche and mind. Hardly any one can escape this money-fever because it pervades the entire structure of a society having reached in its development a nearly terminal stage of inner conflict and 'dis-ease'.

Yet, this stage implies the emergence of most significant, yet not well-understood, possibilities of consciousness transformation. When, in earlier times, money was merely a convenient means of settling the value of exchanged goods, it still had the concrete and physical character of barter. Today money has become the abstract form given to social power—or rather, to social potency. It represents *nothing in particular*, but only *the potentiality* of transforming one's social status and condition of life. Money thus becomes the symbol of potential 'energy' at the socio-cultural level, as currently recognized in the ecological movement which terms it "green energy". In a similar way, 'vitality' (or the life-force within one's total bio-psychic organism) is also potential energy; it is energy available for a great variety of *unspecified* uses.

With the modern type of money, we are therefore dealing with a factor whose universalistic and non-differentiated character makes it similar to what the most recent theories of physics imagine to be the substratum of the physical universe of stars, planets and material objects. Money has become for us a truly *metaphysical* factor, the 'ground' of our socio-cultural existence.

This has very profound and far-reaching consequences. Because of its abstract and undifferentiated character, money (at least in our society) blurs, if not altogether destroys the organic nature of human activity. This activity may, in many instances, still have a functional character insofar as it fills a definite need of the society; but this functional character loses most (and often all) of its meaning and value to the performer of the activity for whom this activity constitutes only a 'job' held for practically the sole purpose of getting money in the form of wages.

Because money is acquired by means of some kind of 'transaction', its acquisition implies some form of social or at least interpersonal relationship. The quantitative aspect of the monetary exchange tends to supersede the qualitative potentiality of the relationship. Socio-cultural transactions and interchanges become almost inevitably determined by the answer to the query, "How much?" Relationships cease to be qualitative when given meaning almost exclusively in terms of money, but function always implies a qualitative factor in the performance of the activity. At the limit we have prostitution; and there is of course intellectual or muscular prostitution when the activity of the mind or the muscles has meaning for the performer only in terms of 'how much' it will bring.

This, perhaps needless to say, fits in well with the character of modern science, because science today deals only with measurements, therefore with numbers and quantitative value. For the physicist, every form of energy can be interpreted in terms of vibratory frequency. For an ordinary man's consciousness, sound and color are basically and vitally different, but for the scientific mind prevalent in our Western society, short-waves differ from x-rays and still more dangerous radiations essentially in terms of their vibratory frequencies. The existential or 'humanistic' consideration of what meaning and value a radiation has for man seeking to actualize his birth-potential in the best manner and the best possible environment is relegated to a secondary position.

The Adwaita type of Hindu metaphysics refers to the world of phenomena as 'maya'. Though this much used and abused word is ordinarily translated as 'illusion', it is etymologically related to the concept of measurement. The world and all its contents can be 'measured', but when an entity or powerful type of energy has value and character only in terms of numbers, it loses its existential meaning, *unless* a qualitative and essential (i.e., super-existential) meaning is given to Number. It is such a meaning that Pythagoras, the Kabballah and related systems of cosmic symbolisms attempted to formulate. In these cosmological systems, Number is given a functional, organic character; a number has a qualitative meaning in terms of the whole cycle of existence whose *phase* it characterizes. Thus in *any* cycle of existence—be it macrocosmic, human or atomic—a phase one or a phase four has an essential, metaphysical significance regardless of the diversity of concrete events or facts to which the phase refers.

This type of thinking, however, has been scorned and is still shunned by our official academic Western mentality, even though a few of the most daring physicists are beginning to move carefully in such a direction, realizing the similarity existing between the Eastern, mystic approach to reality and the latest theories suggested by nuclear physics and its strange, non-rationalistic world. It is indeed important to realize that the nuclear physicist's world of basically unitarian, yet operatively dualistic and bipolar energy has developed parallel to a socio-cultural world in which money is the substratum of an immensely complex global network of human relationships in which, in the final analysis, every activity can be measured, understood and evaluated in terms of 'profit and loss'—of success and failure, or at the religious level, of 'salvation' and 'damnation'.

The profit system and the constant concern with gain and success dominates our Western society. Yet the often quoted paradoxical statement that 'nothing fails like success' points to a very important fact which needs to be emphasized. The dichotomy implied in the modern concept of success and failure does not really apply to a state of culture or religion having an essentially tribal (that is, non-universalistic) character. In such a state a person does the best he can in the position he occupies in terms of birth or obviously demonstrated ability. At the level of functions of the second order, culture takes for granted—or erects into a dogma—that *only a particular and clearly defined set of possibilities is acceptable*. No member of the culture-whole is allowed to question this fact, and very few persons could even think of questioning it, so conditioned people generally are.

This also applies to science and the officially accepted world of science, as long as the intellectual framework of the culture retains its mentally binding power. In modern society, every scientifically conditioned or trained person *knows* that the real world is defined by and limited to what our senses and our rational mind tells us it is. When, a century ago, the concepts of non-Euclidian geometry and, later on, alternative universes took form, this indicated that our Western culture was in the process of breaking down. *A culture breaks down whenever everything becomes possible*—morally, metaphysically, scientifically, and in terms of actual individual behavior. This point cannot be emphasized too strongly.

Individualism is anti-cultural in the sense that it allows a person to challenge the validity of the socio-cultural frame of reference of the culture in which he was born or educated. The 'free' individual theoretically can choose between a variety of alternatives. He is not bound by the imperatives and taboos of his culture. At the very least, he is free to *imagine* alternatives, even non-rational ones. The importance of money, *as used in our present-day society*, is that it enables a wealthy individual not only to imagine alternatives, but in many cases, to act according to what he has imagined. He can break the laws with relative impunity if he can pay for protection. He can travel to various countries and practice different and exotic ways of life. He can change his name and in nearly every way not only think, but behave non-culturally and strictly as a free individual. Nevertheless, in most instances, he is still bound to the ideal of money and usually to the fear of losing it. He may think he is above all moral compulsions and free to do as he pleases, yet most often he remains a willing slave of the fashions of the wealthy. In principle, he should be able to overcome this subservience, but if this is the case, the maintenance of his or her psychological health and balance is a difficult feat. A total non-subservience to *any* collective or group standard causes an often critical state of psychological and emotional tension.

The possibility for such a strictly individualistic and a-cultural freedom has recently been available to the youth of an affluent and permissive society; yet it produced instead what has been called a 'counterculture'. The important and not sufficiently emphasized point is that this counterculture was still a culture—the culture of a group or class of people who, however much they believed in doing "their own thing," nevertheless followed a definite fashion propagated by the ubiquitous media. Just as the very wealthy 'beautiful people' have adopted a fashionable and characteristic way of life, so had the hippies of the sixties. A truly individualized person does not need to feel the *moral reinforcement* of a group; but, I repeat, for most people, it is very difficult to take such an uncompromising stand.

If such a 'liberated' person becomes deeply aware of being essentially related to a group of persons totally self-consecrated to the function of bringing about a *radically different,* more inclusive type of culture and society, then such a human being ceases to be, strictly speaking, a 'free individual'. He has consciously and freely bound himself or herself to a higher type of community—not in terms of a fashion or merely of a generalized and publicized *mood* of revolt, but as the result of a profoundly experienced, deliberate and perhaps heroically sustained decision to work for an alternative form of human existence, thought and felt to be either essentially superior or (in terms of the evolution of humanity) necessary.

Any true culture is 'organic' in the sense that it is based on a limited field of activity—limited in terms of size, acceptable possibilities and well-defined functions. When money comes to entirely dominate a society and its activities, the concept of organic function either vanishes or takes the character of expediency: certain things must be done and whoever is willing to do them for the amount of money society makes available can do them—as a job. But, I repeat, the modern concept of 'job' is non-functional because, in most cases, it does not imply a consciously accepted reference (and even less dedication) to the whole socio-cultural organism. Today, it also becomes identified with the automatic and depersonalizing behavior of machines and with the concept of 'programming'.

Once the various socio-cultural functions cease to operate in a truly organic sense and when groups of people hereditarily or spontaneously attracted to their performance as a 'vocation' lose their defining characteristics, the process of *vulgarization* begins. Today it is rapidly spreading due to the press, radio and TV. Modern means of communication have an ambiguous character. They claim to propagate culture by making the products and ideals of the culture available to the masses which thus are said to become 'educated'; yet, in fact, the media actually devitalize and deteriorate what they vulgarize (from *vulga,* the crowd).

The process of vulgarization is especially important and far-reaching in our present Western civilization, because of the strong ideological emphasis placed on the twin concepts of individualism and egalitarianism. Culture has to be made available to every child and adolescent; but this can only be done by reducing to the lowest common denominator the ideals and concepts on which a particular culture has been based. Egalitarianism is a *spiritual ideal* but not a *cultural reality,* simply because culture, being essentially organic, implies functional differentiation. Similarly, the 18th century concept of the 'individual' refers to an abstraction or, in a spiritual sense, to a transcendental and metaphysical state, *unless* it is given a functional character in terms of a social process. In this case one is dealing with the 'individual-in-his-environment'—that is, with a person functionally related to his society.

The crucial fact emerging from the state of socio-cultural development occurring toward the close of a culture-cycle is that, as all the concepts and values of the culture are becoming vulgarized and dis-functionalized, this process takes place simultaneously with the ever-increasing spread of the products and ideas of *other* cultures through now easily crossed national-cultural frontiers. As these various cultures blend in a kind of mental melting pot, they cease to be truly functional and organic; they become—all of them—a mental humus, a meta-

chemical compost from which the no longer culturally determined minds of relatively 'free' individuals may choose whatever,
at the moment, has the most fascinating appeal to them.

Not all minds are sufficiently developed or free from the harsh
realities imposed by job and family to become deeply acquainted
with unfamiliar and exotic cultures and their philosophies, but
the possibility is open to every 'educated' person. As a result,
the intelligent youth finds himself obsessed by potentiality. He
or she can think, believe, work for almost *anything.* This is an
unparalleled opportunity for consciousness-expansion and, in
some cases, for transcending all sense of bondage to a *particular*
culture and way of life. Yet sooner or later, the youth often discovers that he or she can be bound by not-being-bound, and
depressed by the intoxication of unlimited freedom of choice.
The possibility of radical transformation through deculturalization is open, but it can be deeply upsetting and frightening. Can
one wholesomely accept the process and deculturalization if one
does not know where it will lead? Can one accept chaos and feel
inwardly secure and stable in that acceptance, if one has no
clear vision or indisputable intuition of what is beyond not only
one's culture, but any particular culture—beyond organic living
rooted in biology and functional activity?

In the cultural past, clearly formulated religious patterns of
beliefs and unquestionably valid symbols and images that referred to a transcendental path leading to a spiritual beyond
were not only available but totally accepted as divinely revealed
and unquestionably 'sacred'. The mystically inclined believer
could follow such a path in relative safety even if it meant being
wrenched from the normal biocultural attachments of the social
group in which he was born. This was the only alternative be-
side social normality. But as the last period of a particular
culture is reached and an 'invasion' from other cultures and
life-ideals spread over the entire society, a variety of possibilities
flood the minds of human beings who have been told they are
'free' and that they should lead 'their own' lives as individuals.

If these would-be individuals can somehow manage to get the
magical money that would finance their search, an uncharted
country opens; and their most natural reaction is to look for

old maps of the unknown cultural and religious territory provided by books and the few people who still remember and try to live according to the old directives. The once vitally flourishing culture may still *seem* to flourish, but if so it is almost inevitably due to an artificial isolation which replaces transpersonal creativity by a psychic and aristocratic kind of automatism or at least rigidity. When faced by extinction, the representatives of the perpetuated culture are usually most willing to take disciples. In some outstanding cases, the past-conditioned 'Teacher' or guru, challenged by the psychological and spiritual need of the deculturalized seeker, may become a *transpersonal channel* through which the ancient Source may once more send 'living water'; but this process of transmission entails *personal* difficulties, and deep-seated psychic and emotional resistances are almost unavoidable.

In the great majority of cases, however, neither the *individual* disciple nor the Teacher are truly and radically transformed. In the case of the latter, it is because he cannot let go of the automatism of tradition; the former is likewise untransformed because he is afraid to let go totally, and as a result he (or she) emerges in a highly confused state of mind and quite often returns to the religion and culture of his youth, perhaps with a quasi-fanatical fervor aroused by a deep sense of insecurity. Yet at a *collective* level, the interpenetration between the old culture and the disintegrating society may act somewhat as a *grafting* process, enhancing the possibility of a smoother transition from one phase to another; and this is a most important process.

In any case, the opportunity for individual transformation exists, if not through travel and personal discipleship, then through reading and group contagion. The restless and confused *mind* takes this opportunity out of boredom or emotional rebellion; the daring *will* seizes it, perhaps because it is the only alternative to an impending collapse into unbearable emptiness. To the relatively uneducated mind and the person bound to what appears to be inescapable wage-slavery and/or a substandard social existence, the alternative to resignation and normality may only be some violent form of 'proletarian' revolt. It is usually an empty gesture, but at least the socially deprived and hungry worker has something to rebel against; the very rich capitalist or the executive bound to his frantic rat-race for profit, success and power, in most cases, has no alternative. Psychologically speaking, he is more a slave than the proletarian or the dweller in dehumanizing tenements—a slave to a culture that has uncontrollably fermented into the alcohol of money and led its devotees to inescapable addiction.

A forest during a clear autumnal day can bring to the passer-by a wonderful experience, not only of colorings, but of pungency. The decaying leaves exhale a poignant and almost intoxicating scent. The traveler whose senses are captivated by the scenery and the fragrance of autumn may experience a deep melancholy, overshadowed by the sense of finality and the invisible presence of death. But if he is wise in the awareness of life-rhythms, he may also perceive with awakened spiritual vision the myriad of seeds hidden within the decay of the leaves. His cosmified consciousness may resonate to the counterpoint of death and rebirth, of decay and germination. He should be aware that he too is given the symbolic choice of making of his life a leaf or a seed. This is the autumnal choice, as the cycle of a particular culture-whole is nearing its close—and there are smaller subcycles within the larger collective and racial ones.

What does the choice actually imply? The answer is to be found in the realization that in *any one* seed, the entire power and fate of the whole species to which the plant belongs are brought to *a concrete existential focus*. The seed *is* the whole species in a state of *potential* and focalized activity. The seed is the utterly consecrated agent of the species; its existence has a 'transpersonal' quality, not in the sense that it operates *beyond* the concrete reality of the physical realm of single and separate entities—that is, of persons, if we think of the human species—but in the sense that the seed is simply a focalizing instrumentality *through* which (*trans*) the species will act, if the time and place are favorable.

This transpersonal character of the symbolic 'seed person' reveals that the functions of the fourth order are definitely and irrevocably operative in the man or woman who, through a determined and sustained act of self-consecration has achieved a radical metamorphosis of whatever for him or her is implied in the state of 'being-in-the-world'. The metamorphosis requires the process of deculturalization as a primary factor; and it is only when the historical time has arrived allowing this process to gain a collective social, cultural and political momentum that individuals can *spontaneously* resonate and become deliberately attuned to it.

Before such a time, during the early periods of the culture-whole's development, such a metamorphosis demands special conditions. The Teacher, who then is a member of a more or less secret Brotherhood, has to seek out and select one who, after a very drastic training and testing, might prove able to take his place. Today, in our Western world, a great many would-be disciples are seeking willing and ready 'Teachers'. But at any time, the Gospel's injunction remains the indisputable condition for total metamorphosis and truly transpersonal living: "Be ye separate!"—for as Jesus said to his disciples: "You are *in* the world, but not *of* the world." The seed must leave the plant that bore it before it can operate, even potentially, as a seed—but 'leaving' here does not necessarily mean an act of physical separation. What matters is an inner and irreversible act of *severance*.

In the last phase of a culture-whole, an antiphonal situation develops: the self-consecrated 'seed-man' or woman *consciously* grows into seed-immortality while the 'mass-man' *unconsciously* slides into a collective state of psychic disintegration. The latter category includes the very rich as well as the proletarian; because what characterizes it is an utter dependence upon money and all that money is expected to provide. This state of dependency is as dominant a feature of the psyche of the wealthy executive or socialite hypnotized by profit, money-power or the fear of losing social status dependent upon money, as it is a haunting necessity in the existence of the tens of millions of factory and office workers for whom, according to the style of living now popular, the loss of a job can be catastrophic.

It is the craving by the wealthy for an unsatisfiable (because abstract and self-multiplying) money power, as well as the yearning by the masses of educated working people—indoctrinated with the great Western ideals of individual freedom, equality, self-expression and material abundance for all, yet at least partially deprived of the concrete manifestation of these ideals—that is bringing the development of our Euro-American culture-whole to a state of acute crisis. Because, in the process of industrialization, Western people have had to conquer the regions in which older cultures were slowly disintegrating or remained in a static, quasi-fossilized condition, the crisis has now a world-wide character. It has become a biospheric crisis as well as a social and political crisis, equally affecting the conquerors and the conquered people.

The only basic and permanent way in which either a gradual or a sudden catastrophe can be avoided is if a sufficient number of self-consecrated individuals succeed in developing within their total being functions of the fourth order—compassion, holistic thinking and the capacity to clearly envision and indomitably as well as effectively work for a new and global culture-whole. It can still be a culture-whole if it encompasses the entire planet, because the Earth is a limited organic field of activity. But it must be a culture-whole whose essential feature is an all-human inclusiveness, and whose collective operations will manifest an essential harmony of clearly defined functions performed in the creative mode of the 'sacred'.

Today we may only be able to dream of such a plenary and harmonic-polyphonic society; and there can be no assurance that even our children or great-grandchildren will be able to actually participate in it. Yet if the vision is not given form, at least at the level of concepts and concretizable ideals, there may be no possibility of avoiding a deep regression to the biological-cultural level of tribal organization; and this would mean that mankind would have to begin again at nearly the bottom of the cultural ladder. Even if this should prove to be inescapable, it is certain that if, during the Fall of the year, seeds have not sown themselves in the midst of the decaying leaves, there will be no vegetation when spring begins.

6

THE IDEAL OF SOCIAL PLENITUDE

After a long historical period of *differentiation* needed for the development of the several basic types of human beings—and many more secondary types, each of them proficient in the performance of characteristic functions—one may hope for an age of *synthesis*. In that age, the incessant conflicts of temperament and interests which have marked the successive ascendancies of each of the main human types should be pacified and transcended; peace and harmony should reign among assuaged individuals at last aware of the interrelatedness and interdependence of all the individualized forms and modes of activity mankind has been able to develop.

We assuredly cannot be certain that this potential and expectable phase of synthesis in the evolution of human societies will be experienced in a world deeply disturbed, but also dynamized, by the global impact of our Western civilization; the coming generations may witness a catastrophic miscarriage, or even accept the necessity of an abortion, should a monstrous future be expectable. Moreover, we cannot say what form a peaceful and all-inclusive global society *would* take, if it is relatively smoothly born; yet many visionary minds have tried to formulate, at least along broad lines, what form it *should* take, according to their own ideal of human fulfillment. The name given to these ideal forms of society is *utopia*.

Utopias have a profound meaning and value as catalytic agents. To the alert and aware mind they show what direction the evolution of humanity might take if certain principles of organization were successful in polarizing and unifying the hopes and the wills of the most dynamic individuals now living or about to be born. Because the utopia-builders do not completely agree on what these principles should be, the utopias present us with alternatives. They help us realize what our particular philosophies of existence and our approaches to individual problems imply, once they are brought into concrete form and generalized as collective ways of life. And if our minds are concerned with the practical, social, political, cultural, and religious realities now existing all over the globe, these utopian ideals force us to consider the manner in which they could become actualities.

What is possible tomorrow depends upon what the many yesterdays have brought to the present world-situation. Our endeavor to actualize the possible future is also inevitably conditioned by the kind of interpretation we have given to the tumultuous events and the often tragic conflicts of past centuries. This in turn depends on the way our minds conceive the whole process of human evolution on our planet—its initial phases giving a clue to its probable conclusion, if we believe in an ordered and significant world-process.

a. *Materialistic and Spirit-Oriented Utopias*

If we think of the development of mankind in purely materialistic terms and we see it taking place in an exclusively physical universe in which force acts against force and rigid laws prevail in a manner essentially definable by our rational intellect, then the utopia we imagine may well be one of the Marxist-type implying a kind of leveling down of mankind into a classless society dominated by problems of productivity and material organization. It may also be the type of technocratic utopia imagined by a scientific mentality glorifying the empiricism and intellectualism of our Western society and, deliberately or not, leading to the totalitarian rule of a class of managers, engineers, biologists, psychologists and medical men attempting to build a 'perfect' type of human beings and an environment befitting their concept of flawless functioning and total health, happiness and prosperity. Whether such a concept could become actualized in a viable society living in a healthful biosphere is, of course, a question that no one can answer; no more than one can deduce from what has happened in Soviet Russia and China whether the pure Communist ideal would ever be possible, considering the manner in which egocentrically individualized human beings act today.

At the other end of the philosophical spectrum, we have what could be called the 'spiritual' utopias based on the idea that man is essentially a spiritual being operating in and through a physical organism, but not necessarily bound by or even consciously attached to it. While the materialistic utopias tend to stress the collective factor in human development—or at least the concept of objectivity—the spiritual philosopher and mystically inclined person emphasize the individual and his subjective experiences that reveal the possibility of the endless superphysical development of a spiritual 'essence', a permanent 'I'-consciousness. There are several basic kinds of spiritual philosophies, some attempting to present a 'monistic' approach usually leading to an explicit, or at least implicit, kind of theistic religion; others giving a 'pluralistic' and either 'personalistic' or 'monadic' type of spiritual foundation to the universe. Each of these philosophical or metaphysical approaches could lead to a utopian ideal of society; and I can only mention here the kind of utopia which the great Indian seer-philosopher, poet, and yogi—Sri Aurobindo—envisioned at the close of his most impressive work, *The Life Divine*.[1]

In the last chapters of the book, "The Gnostic Individual" and "The Gnostic Life", Aurobindo evoked the emergence of "gnostic" individuals totally consecrated to, and manifesting in their transformed personalities the "supermental Truth" and radiance of Ishvara—the unitary Source of our universe. He foresaw the emergence of "gnostic communities" formed by such individuals. After his death, his companion and associate in the 'great work' of human transformation, Mother Mira, actually started what is meant to become such a community in Auroville, near Pondicherry, India—and the work is slowly proceeding since her passing away.

Aurobindo's vision of a "supermental or gnostic race of beings"

---

[1] The contents of this work appeared in their original form in a long series of essays published in the magazine *Arya*, begun in 1914. A revised edition appeared in New York in 1950, and it is now included in the monumental series of some thirty volumes constituting the complete works of Sri Aurobindo (Aurobindo Ashram, Pondicherry, India).

is most inspiring. "The gnostic individual would be the consummation of the spiritual man; his whole way of being, thinking, living, acting would be governed by the power of a vast universal spirituality. . . . All his existence would be fused into oneness with the transcendent and universal Self and Spirit; all his action would originate from and obey the Supreme Self and Spirit's divine governance of Nature. . . . All beings would be to him his own selves, all ways and powers of consciousness would be felt as the ways and powers of his own universality." Yet Aurobindo also adds that "a supramental or gnostic race of beings would not be a race made according to a single type, molded by a single fixed pattern, for the law of the supermind is unity fulfilled in diversity. Therefore there would be an infinite diversity in the manifestation of the gnostic consciousness, although this consciousness would still be one in its basis, in its constitution, in its all-revealing and all-uniting order."[2]

Sri Aurobindo briefly indicates that in the process of actualizing such an ideal of "divine living", there would be people still unable to reach such a gnostic state, clinging to what he calls "the Ignorance", the dark realm of egos, conflicts and frustrations, but so far as I know he did not present a clear picture of what would be the relationship between the different levels of beings, nor did he outline what might be the transitional structure of a society that, in time, would lead to such a world-wide gnostic humanity. This is the problem that Indian metaphysicians and seers have been unready or unwilling to tackle, so strong has been, for millennia, their one-pointed concentration on the spiritual development of the individual.

Today, however, and from the point of view I have taken in this book, it is important to interpret this characteristically Indian approach in terms of the relationship between socio-cultural and individual factors—that is, between the collective and the individual polarities in human existence. In proclaiming the supremacy of the 'liberated' individual spirit and its identity with the universal Self, the seers of the Upanishad period sought a psychological way to compensate for, and in a sense neutralize,

---

[2] Sri Aurobindo, *The Life Divine* (original edition) pp. 862-863, Chp. 27, "The Gnostic Being".

the collectivistic pressure of a society that, since the Brahmin caste had come to control it (after the famous and more or less mythical War, the end of which traditionally marked the beginning of Kali Yuga), had become rigidly planned and ritualized in the extreme. Whenever and wherever the collective factor overpowerfully dominates an existential situation, sooner or later the individual factor has to assert itself, and it asserts itself in a manner which befits the character of the people involved.

Because, in pre-Buddhist India, the rationalistic, analytical, and objective mind (the functions of the third order) had not yet developed to any real degree of effectiveness—except in special and isolated cases—the psychological compensation for the crystallizing and binding collectivism of the Indian society had to take the form of withdrawal into a subjective and mystical state of consciousness. Also, because the power of biological urges was very strong in tropical India, it had to be controlled by physical disciplines; these disciplines, broadly covered by the term 'yoga', were devised for the use of individuals and related to the development of subjective experiences. Yoga represents an essentially, and in many instances totally, individualized mode of existence utterly consecrated to the one supreme Individual, Ishvara; and, as I have previously mentioned, Ishvara (or Ish) is the *unity aspect* of the cosmos, its original condition or Source.

When, in the Europe of the early Renaissance, a profound movement of revolt against the oppressive dogmatism of the Medieval Catholic order spread, it could use as leverage the ancient background of the Greek rationalism and objectivism. Greek culture had stressed the value of the concrete, objective experience of the Beautiful; it had worshipped reason and a sense of proportion (thus of formal relationship) and to some extent developed the analytical power of the human intellect. For this reason, and also because the Church powerfully claimed complete control over whatever referred to a transcendental religious concept of spirituality, the individualistic revolt against Medieval collectivism turned into a glorification of the rational and analytical intellect, of scientific empiricism and materialistic technology.

A rationalistic individualism seeks to prove its validity by *objective* reasons and experimental facts which the collective mentality has to accept because it can use them to increase its material well-being. On the other hand, a mystical kind of individualism gains strength and finds its apotheosis in *subjective* experiences in which the human individual identifies himself in consciousness with the cosmic Individual, the supreme Self. It is evident that such experiences of identification generate a power and charisma that fascinates the collective mind; and now our scientists and psychologists are busy quantitatively measuring and trying to find an intellectual explanation for what takes place in the body and the psyche when such mystical experiences occur. The experiences occur when the centralizing individual factor in the consciousness of human beings *almost* completely overpowers the socio-cultural and organic-biological collective factor in human nature, allowing the consciousness to be fully attuned to that of the universal Self, center of the universal Whole. If the 'overpowering' were total, what we interpret as 'reaching Nirvana' would occur.

A purely 'gnostic' humanity would represent humanity at the threshold of Nirvana, or what Teilhard de Chardin envisioned as the omega state of total union with Christ, the divine Individual. This may be the final consummation of humanity, the "Seventh Race . . . a Race of Buddhas and Christs" of which H. P. Blavatsky speaks in *The Secret Doctrine* (Sixth Adyar Edition, 1971, Vol. iii, p. 413). But it seems quite impossible to conceive of such a consummation except in the most distant future, and I would add, most likely on a *transphysicalized* Earth.

Sri Aurobindo's gnostic ideal should therefore be thought of as being a goal applicable in any foreseeable future only to 'gnostic communities'. These, if they succeed in maintaining their existence at a level at least approximating the vision of the great Indian seer, could influence the surrounding masses of mankind and act as a new kind of 'apostolic Brotherhood'; but the rigor of the commitment implied in Aurobindo's, integral (purna) *yoga* (which can be translated as plenary identification through total self-surrender to the Divine) may throw some doubt on the successful exteriorization of such a spiritual ideal on a wide scale, unless some unprecedented (but most likely) cataclysmic process of planet-wide transformation occurs.

b. *The Plenary Society*

What I have written in the past (particularly in *We Can Begin Again—Together*, in 1970) concerning the possibility of a future state of global organization of mankind represents an attempt to deal with the actual psychological facts of human existence, and to do so unemotionally and without the prejudices inherited from over two centuries of Euro-American ideology. It is also an attempt to think of the organization of such a global society, not exclusively in terms of human factors, but also in relation to the basic telluric, climatic, and regional features of the entire globe—a 'geomorphic' (but not 'geopolitical'!) approach. I shall not deal here with the last point which I have hinted at in my book, *Modern Man's Conflicts: The creative challenge of a global society.*[3] All I can do here is to present a few basic principles, which are directly related to the ideas discussed in the preceding chapters of this book.

The concept of what I have called a *plenary* society rests upon the idea that a human being is an organized field of functional activities and that these activities manifest at four levels when fully operative (a relatively rare case at this time). A four-level type of functional activity tends to produce an equally fourfold kind of socio-cultural organization in order to meet the needs of different types or levels of human development, each type naturally seeking to emphasize in its own way of life one level of functions over another.

This differentiation of levels of functional activity should be considered a *natural* and thoroughly acceptable and justifiable tendency even in terms of socio-cultural organization. But—and this is an absolutely essential point—functional activity is *not* the only factor to be considered. As I have stated early in this book (cf. p. 11 ff), wherever there are organized fields of activity

---

[3] Written in 1945, published in New York in 1948, and now long out of print.

there is also consciousness. This consciousness may exist in a *diffuse* state, belonging to the system-as-a-whole rather than to a particular exemplar; or it may be *centralized* and take the potential or only partially actualized and independent form of 'I-consciousness'. This I-consciousness characterizes the *human* state of individuality, and individuality implies at least a relative sense of responsibility and inner freedom of the 'will'—the individual's capacity to mobilize energy according to a conscious desire, intention or purpose.

Where individuality and the decision-making faculty exist, human life should be understood in two ways: in terms of centralized I-consciousness, and in terms of functional activity. Once the third order of functions (the individualizing functions) operates with some degree of efficacy in human beings, two realms of human existence have to be considered: the essentially subjective realm of *individuality* in which every individual is (in principle) unique and (at least potentially) self-determined because essentially 'free'; and the objective realm of *functionality* in which the activity of a particular person (body and psyche) is intrinsically related to the activities of whatever is active around him—whether it be other human beings, animals, plants or any other factor in the organic existence of the planet: air and atmospheric currents, rivers, sea, fields of magnetism or radiation, etc.

Unless these two realms of human existence are clearly differentiated—even though they evidently interact and interpenetrate at every point and at all times—no social system can harmoniously exist and fulfill all the needs of mankind. The basic problem, however, is *how* a society and its culture will be able (1) to define the boundaries, and especially the interactions between the two realms, and (2) to organize in a *collectively efficient yet individually acceptable and fulfilling manner* the various types of activities required for the harmonious and optimal operation of *all* human functions. These functions operate at the levels of matter, life, and mind; and their operation today cannot be considered truly and fully 'human' unless they allow for the development of the individualized consciousness in the best possible manner at any particular future stage of human evolution.

The plenary society I have envisioned is one in which, while *spiritual equality* indisputably and actually would be recognized as the fact of social existence, *functional differentiation* would also be the basis on which the society would be organized. And the entire system of social organization would have as its aim the welfare of the whole of humanity and the fulfillment of the essential purpose of human evolution on this planet.

The basic 'holarchic' principle implied here is that the fulfillment of the purpose of a whole under optimal conditions is more important than the welfare and happiness of the parts of that whole. But a part is also a whole containing many parts; and as a whole the fulfillment of its own nature and purpose is also essential. This holarchic principle implies therefore a relativism of values. The basic problem it poses arises from the need to reconcile—or more exactly, *to harmonize and give a creative meaning* to the relationship between—the two principles of holarchic organization.

The principle of 'individuality' and that of 'effective functional differentiation' would require almost inevitably a constant effort to harmonize as long as each individual participant in the whole life of humanity had not reached a full development of functions of the fourth order—thus the development not only of an unpossessive and all-encompassing kind of Christ-love and Buddha-compassion, but of the 'clear mind' that perceives the true relationship of every part of a whole to every other part, and also of the 'selfless will' that can operate only when such a 'cosmic' mind apprehends the 'Truth' (or dharma) of the whole. This is why, in my book, *We can Begin Again—Together* (Part Two, Chapter 8: "A Holarchic Approach to World Organization", pp. 141-174), I stressed the principle of a threefold pattern of social organization and the need to recognize, accept, and allow for the operation of three basic types of social functions, each of which calls for a natural type of human consciousness and operative ability.

Briefly said, there are human beings who, by nature and through their entire life-span, feel strongly attached to the land on which they were born and to the culture which molded their feeling and mental responses to life—and I see no reason to believe that this type of person, which today probably consti-

tutes eight- or nine-tenths of the world's population, will disappear from the surface of the globe, at least not for the foreseeable future. I have spoken of such persons as regionalists, or
as 'culture-men' (or women) whose natural capacities and life-
goal are *to produce*—whether what is produced is food or products of various kinds. Their produtive activity is most satisfac-
torily and happily performed when in harmonious relationship,
on the one hand, with nature and its seasonal rhythms, and on
the other, with a particular culture and its traditional manifestations. In the past, one thought of this type of human being
mainly as peasants and artisans; but the type should include all
those whose activities are deeply conditioned by local, racial,
and ethnic characteristics. When deprived of their rootedness in
a particular broadly geographical and socio-cultural environment
—which also includes a particular form of traditional religion—
these people actually become disoriented and live a disharmonic
existence, as is the case today in our enormous and chaotic cities.

The other and contrasting type of human beings—the universalist or 'civilization-man' (or woman)—does not feel, or has
overcome at a relatively early age, a strong or significant attachment to the particular region of his birth, or to his family,
race, environment, and culture. The mind of these individuals
carries the life-accent; they tend to be proud of, or at least
strongly reliant upon, their own development and their intellectual and organizing capacities. They are the typical managers,
organizers, promoters, and executives, at ease while dealing with
relatively large and complex 'systems'. They find their innate
nature fulfilled in large-scale organization—and, at the conceptual level, with building new theories, or ever more inclusive
systems of philosophy and religious interpretation. They are
often hyperactive individuals, resentful of physical, earthly limitations; they tend to rebel impulsively against any kind of subservience to the requirements of strictly particular situations,
and are often impatient with people whose visions and concerns
are narrowly defined by biopsychic temperament and cultural
tradition.

Any plenary society should not only have recognized and accepted the co-existence of these two fundamental types of human beings, but should have become organized in such a way that the two types are able to fulfill their respective natures and capacities in a state of harmonious cooperation. This would require a basic understanding of the character and purpose of this natural two-level differentiation of human activity, leading to a 'live-and-let-live' attitude. It would necessitate the realization by all human beings that each function has its place and meaning in the harmonious workings of the whole society—which, in the future, would mean the whole of humanity.

However, it would be too unrealistic to believe that the two types would easily reach and maintain such a superpersonal and holistic understanding; and particularly that, while working together on specific problems of relationship among economic, social, or cultural factors—a relationship which each type naturally tends to interpret according to its own temperament—their decisions would not conflict. It is therefore evident that there will be a basic need for the exercise of a function to be performed by human beings best adapted to its requirements. These individuals would be the 'harmonizers'; they would naturally be found among individuals in whom the fourth order of functions would be developed—just as the universalist type of civilization-man would naturally refer to individuals in whom functions of the third order would greatly predominate, perhaps at the expense of functions of the first and second orders. It is impossible to definitely picture how these 'harmonizers' would operate, but they certainly would have to be closely involved in situations in which any potential conflict of interest between the two other types could be expected to arise.

In other words, the plenary society I envision would find a proper place and function for three essential types of human beings. It would accept *functional differentiation* as a basis for harmonious cooperation; yet it would also consider as fundamental the principle of *spiritual equality*—or to use a popular phrase, 'the worth and dignity of the human person'. Functional differentiation would imply the actual—and not merely theoretical and hypocritically proclaimed—'equality of opportunity' allowing every newborn to naturally and spontaneously discover the level of operation, and within that level the special function, which constitutes his or her *dharma* or 'truth of being'.

c. The Relative Failure of Western Society

How to determine which individual person *naturally* belongs to which basic type of function is evidently a difficult problem at the present state of human evolution and consciousness; yet it should be interesting to note that the political life of the United States is based on a somewhat similar differentiation of the legislative, the executive (with all its various departments and modes of social control), and the judiciary. Unfortunately, this threefold principle of organization is understood only at the political level of *power*, and in terms of 'checks and balances' in the use of that power. The threefold principle should be seen operating as well, and more basically, at the level of the individualized *consciousness* of the people belonging to the sociocultural whole.

At this level, no sane and objective person would deny the existence of fundamental and natural differences between the needs, desires and goals of individuals. Any attempt to eradicate and bring to a level of uniformity these psychological differences —related to differences in biopsychic temperament *yet transcending them*—is doomed to failure. What should be done instead is —I repeat—to allow each basic mode of functional activity to unfold according to its own rhythm and at its most characteristic, most productive, and most meaningful level, yet within the limitations of the special character of the whole in which it participates.

An example of the possibility of plenary multi-level group organization can be drawn from the world of music; for in the great motets of the early Renaissance we have an archetypal presentation of an evolving organization according to which four or eight melodic lines flow together in relative independence in polyphonic interplay. Yet this *polyphonic* structure is also *har-*

monic, for all the notes of the motet belong to one particular 'tonality', representing the principle of socio-cultural integration.

Our classical European culture nevertheless was unable to bring such a model of organization to a condition of plenary fulfillment because the composers of the motets paid too much attention to the intellectual element of the rigidly determined 'form' of the whole. They stressed the abstract and quantitative character rather than the livingness and quality of the musical units—the notes—because the men and women who sang these notes were not allowed by their dogmatic religion or their politically totalitarian society to develop their potential of experience and self-actualization as fully individualized and richly living human beings.

The same thing occurred at the socio-political level during the 18th century when the men of "the Enlightenment"—a very restricted and intellectualized enlightenment!—could only think of 'democracy' in terms of an equally abstract and quantitative egalitarianism, while glorifying "Reason" and a mechanistic vision of a purely material universe. The legacy of such a socio-cultural philosophy inevitably produced the critical situation the whole of mankind is now facing. It had to be critical because the intellectual and individualizing functions of the third order were given, at least in theory, a nearly exclusive kind of prominence which perverted the nature of the functions of the first and second orders, and made it extremely difficult for the functions of the fourth order to play a significant and transformative role. Thus, because the intellect operates most spectacularly in the realm of physical matter which it can freely analyze and manipulate, we have inherited, together with increased physical well-being, the curse of unbridled industrialization and of a quantitative type of existence measured by statistics and balance-sheets in which the human person is merely a number, unrelated to functional activity and, what is more, to a particular state of consciousness and potentiality.

The plenary society I envision can only validly and successfully operate if, in terms of the dialectical process of human evolution, it truly constitutes a *synthesis;* and a true synthesis has to include—in a harmonized, transformed, and repolarized condition—all that was added to the original thesis during the phase of antithesis. What was added during the Age of Differentiation and Conflicts (the four basic stages of which were outlined in the preceding chapter) is essentially a fully conscious, sharply defined, precisely effective and clearly transferable realization of the place and purpose of physical and psychological human activities—in all their forms—and also of the negative possibilities material existence presents to a centralizing core of consciousness. When this core of consciousness has to operate in the midst of the type of *physical/material* conditions found in the Earth's biosphere, and as the centralizing and individualizing center for biological energies, it almost inevitably functions at first as an exclusivistic, possessive, proud, yet insecure ego. It is only when—after many serious and perhaps devastating crises and much suffering—functions of the fourth order begin to operate that the true individualizing center, the "I", can be heard without 'static' induced by disharmonic brain activity.

Only then can the individual person find his or her place within the 'greater Whole' of humanity—a whole seen for the first time as an integral but immensely complex *organism*. It is an organic Whole, but because it is 'human' it has within itself the possibility of radically transforming itself. There is no fate-ordained dead end for humanity, no more than for the individual center of consciousness within any human being. Activity may cease when the limiting boundary of its cycle at a particular level is reached; but the mind-seed of consciousness is drawn into the field of operation of the greater whole of which it has been a focalized form of expression.

The concepts of fullness of harmonic activity—what I call 'plenitude' of being—should not imply the idea of finality. A holistic philosophy of activity can accept neither absolute end nor beginning. Time is cyclic. Space is infinite. Motion unceasing. Whatever reaches the state of plenitude—be it an individual person, mankind-as-a-whole, or a galaxy—finds itself at the threshhold of emptiness. The consciousness that truly experiences plenitude, in that very moment, must know the ineradicable longing for greater fullness of being within a larger field of activity. The potentiality of rebirth is inherent in every death; but as far as we know, only human beings—and beings greater than man—can, for an instant, consciously perceive in a flash of light the potency of rebirth in the darkness of the closing cycle of physical existence.

Christian mystics have spoken of the "Dark Night of the Soul" that so often follows great experiences of union with the Divine—when every mode of activity is drawn into the center of the human field and a self-transcending contact is established between this center and the center of an all-encompassing Greater Whole to which we attribute the character of divinity. Buddhist philosophers stress the experience of the Void. This Dark Night, this Void, are the unavoidable polarities of the experience of illumination and plenitude. But in that moment, when the feeling of plenitude changes into the hollow sense of emptiness, the potentiality of rebirth is released. In most cases, however, the formation of consciousness and the activity patterns that led to the moment of plenitude oppose a strong power of inertia to the movement toward rebirth. A more or less long period of disintegration of the past therefore has to follow.

We have seen this process at work during the periods of transition between the various stages of development of the individual person and of human society. But when the fourth order of functions are fully developed in a person, and the now only ideal state of truly plenary society is reached, this will not be the end. The Earth itself is but a part of the solar system; and encompassing all solar systems is the galaxy. Still beyond, the present cosmos of which we are physically aware extends. Moreover, there undoubtedly are other states of substance beyond what we call physical matter. There are other modes of activity and forms of consciousness now inconceivable to us.

Ultimately, we have to postulate infinity as *That out of which all finite fields of activity emerge*. We have to do so intellectually as long as we think in terms of change, activity, relationship between wholes of existence and therefore time, space, and motion. We may also 'feel' the mysterious 'Presence' of infinity, not only surrounding but pervading us, in moments of radical transformation when our deepest sense of finiteness collapses, and we find ourselves shipwrecked in the immense Ocean of potentiality.

In such moments, the devoted Christian finds strength in the Biblical assertion that "with God all things are possible." There are many ways of envisioning "God." Essentially, for whomever believes in the validity of the cyclocosmic world-view presented here, God is the undefeatable and ever-present power of transformation that makes it possible for smaller fields of activity and consciousness to become transformed into ever vaster fields. God is also the power which insures that every release of cosmic and life energy occurs as a unit within which a structural principle operates, maintaining that unit whole and endowing it with consciousness. To operate as a harmoniously functioning whole; to transform oneself stage after stage according to the encompassing rhythm of a Greater Whole; and to be able to do so consciously through a mysterious attunement of one's center with the center of the Greater Whole: this is the meaning and challenge of human existence.

INDEX

Activity, 11, 12, 36; differentiated as function, 13, 133; relationship to wholeness and consciousness, 27, 133, 140; at sociocultural level, 30; cessation of, 140

agape, 40

Age of Differentiation and Conflicts, 89, 92, 94, 96, 103, 109, 140. *See also* Antithesis

American Indian, 97

Anthropologgy, function of, 79

Antithesis, 17, 89, 97, 109. *See also* Age of Differentiation and Conflicts

Aristotle, 108

Assagioli, Roberto, 9

Atlantis, 39, 81, 91

Atman, 63

Sri Aurobindo, 12, 42, 129, 132

Avatar, 104, 105

Being and Non-Being, 12

Bergson, Henri, 27

Biblical References, 49, 83, 125, 142

Biology, as foundation, 14; and Culture, 25, 28, 38, 56, 59, 66, 90, 93. *See also* First Order (of) Functions

Biological Functions, 13, 21, 23; relationship to social functions, 24, 25, 28, 57, 66, 69, 82; difference between sex and other, 52; and marriage, 59; relationship to process of individualization, 66, 88; and Spirit, 30, 38, 89, 106; and transition to Culture, 15, 21, 22, 28, 90, 92; and ego, 34, 113. *See also* First Order (of) Functions

Biological Level, 42, 48, 88, 97, 103, 107, 109, 110; functioning at, 13;

relationship at, 23; consciousness at, 34; sex at, 53. *See also* First Order (of) Functions

Blavatsky, H. P., 73, 80

Bodhisattva Ideal, 39, 48, 50

Brahman, 12, 63

Budda, Buddhism, 39, '71, 132, 135, 141

Caesar Image, 58, 64, 101

Capra, Fritjof, 29

Center. *See* Consciousness, centering of

Chi, 13

China, 100

Change, 10, 44, 47

Christ, 58, 104, 109, 132; Image, 64, 101, 103; cosmic, 41; -gift, 40; -love, 50, 69, 135. *See also* Jesus

Christianity, Christian tradition, 12, 40, 41, 58, 59, 102

Circumcision, 57

Civilization, 29; process of, 28; origin of, 80; -man or -woman, 136

Collective Factor (or Polarity), of human nature, 3-8, 14, 16, 18, 79, 129, 132, 134

Collective, person, 8; personality, 113

Collective Unconscious, 4

Commerce, developmental function of, 94, 98, 109

Consciousness, 11, 13, 26, 27; relationship to ego, 34; and activity, 11, 44; and mind, 27; and wholeness, 11, 27, 34; at tribal level, 65; I-consciousness, 134; social, 23; and relatedness, 24; at biological level, 64; evolution of, 29,

Other Quest Books –

ABRIDGEMENT OF THE SECRET DOCTRINE
By H. P. Blavatsky.
Edited by E. Preston and C. Humphreys
The creation of the universe and the evolution of man.

BEING, EVOLUTION, AND IMMORTALITY
By Haridas Chaudhuri
Insights into the mystery of being.

CULTURE, CRISIS, AND CREATIVITY
By Dane Rudhyar
The myth of our cultural omnipotence, omniscience, and permanence.

H. P. BLAVATSKY AND THE SECRET DOCTRINE
Edited by Virginia Hanson
An anthology on Blavatsky's contribution to world thought.

MAN, GOD, AND THE UNIVERSE
By I.K. Taimni
A spiritual-philosophical examination of creation.

OCCULT PREPARATIONS FOR A NEW AGE
By Dane Rudhyar
A contemporary commentary on *The Secret Doctrine* of H. P. Blavatsky.

Available from
QUEST BOOKS
306 W. Geneva Road
Wheaton, Illinois 60187